THE DRINKER'S ADDICTION

ADDICTION

Its Nature and
Practical Treatment

THE DRINKER'S ADDICTION

Its Nature and Practical Treatment

By

FRANCIS T. CHAMBERS, JR.

Philadelphia, Pennsylvania

With a Foreword by

Kenneth E. Appel, M.D.

Professor Emeritus
Former Chairman
Department of Psychiatry
School of Medicine
University of Pennsylvania
Philadelphia, Pennsylvania

CHARLES C THOMAS · PUBLISHER
Springfield · Illinois · U.S.A.

Published and Distributed Throughout the World by

CHARLES C THOMAS • PUBLISHER

BANNERSTONE HOUSE

301-327 East Lawrence Avenue, Springfield, Illinois, U.S.A.

NATCHEZ PLANTATION HOUSE

735 North Atlantic Boulevard, Fort Lauderdale, Florida, U.S.A.

With THOMAS BOOKS *careful attention is given to all details of manufacturing and design. It is the Publisher's desire to present books that are satisfactory as to their physical qualities and artistic possibilities and appropriate for their particular use.* THOMAS BOOKS *will be true to those laws of quality that assure a good name and good will.*

Printed in the United States of America

RN-1

To

My Wife

FOREWORD

This book, *The Drinker's Addiction,* should be un-
usually useful to a large number of people in our
country—to those involved personally in the difficulties,
entanglements and problems of alcohol addiction and to their
families, relatives, friends, employers and family physicians.
This is one of the largest social and health problems in the
United States. It involves millions of people directly or
indirectly. It is related to personal, family, and business
frustrations and failures, marital suffering, agony and breakdown. The extensiveness of the problems and ramifications
can scarcely be realized, whether human, personal or
financial.

It is rare that one finds a book with such practical recom-
mendations and which is so easily understood. It comes from
a man with extensive and successful experience. It has a
down-to-earth quality which makes it easily comprehended
by the layman. I recommend it heartily.

Although the use of alcohol, as well as its abuse, dates
back to the beginning of recorded time, the effects of its
excessive use did not even have an acceptable name until
mid-nineteenth century when the word *alcoholism* was
coined. Even after this recognition of the condition, there
was little accomplished in prevention, control and treatment
of alcoholism until the enlightenment of the twentieth
century, particularly the last thirty years. In this time our
society has gradually moved toward the acceptance of

vii

alcoholism as an illness, an illness that can be treated. The founding of Alcoholics Anonymous; the development of the Yale (now Rutgers) Center for Studies on Alcohol; the statement of the American Medical Association affirming the disease concept of alcoholism; the court decisions that the alcoholic is a patient to be treated and not a criminal to be punished, and, now, most recently, the establishment by the Federal Government of the National Center for Prevention and Control of Alcoholism:* all of these historic steps have brought us closer to the probability of an eventual decrease in the incidence of alcoholism.

In the meantime, in spite of these welcome indications of progress, there is still much ground to be covered. Until recently the incidence of alcoholism has, through the years, shown a steady increase. Whether this is an actual increase in the numbers of alcoholics, or whether, with the removal of some of the stigma related to alcoholism, more people are coming out in the open and asking for help, is relatively unimportant. What *is* important is the fact that alcoholism, which for years has been considered the fourth major public health problem in the United States, has now displaced cancer from third place, and is exceeded in importance only by cardiac, circulatory diseases, and mental illness.

Inroads against alcoholism have been attempted on all fronts: physiological, biochemical, psychological and "social"; treatment, research and education. As an integral part of the latter, in the last ten years there has been a substantial amount of material published in the field of alcoholism. One might ask whether another book is needed. *This* book should enrich the current literature. The author writes from two frames of reference: 1) from the wealth of his own experience working in conjunction with an eminent and extraordinarily successful psychiatrist, Dr. Edward A. Strecker, with whom Mr. Chambers was a co-author of an important book,

*See paragraph four and footnote in the author's preface.

Alcohol: One Man's Meat, in the treatment of alcoholism; and in recent years working in collaboration with the psychiatric staff at the Institute of the Pennsylvania Hospital, Philadelphia, Pennsylvania, a private psychiatric hospital; and 2) from his own personal experience as a former alcoholic.

Written for the layman, the book offers in simple language needed information about alcoholism, treatment for the alcoholic himself, for his family members, friends and family doctor. For every victim of his own alcoholism, there are estimated to be three or four other persons equally "victimized" by it. Because there are not nearly enough professionally trained people to work in this field, it becomes vitally important that the average layman understand the problems of the illness and its treatment. The author makes this understanding available by presenting alcoholism in its proper perspective: growing out of the developmental hazards of childhood; uniquely different from individual to individual; and responding differently to various therapeutic methods. Thus, this book should prove valuable in disseminating more widely among the general public and general practitioners a practical knowledge of alcoholism and its treatment.

For his determination and constructive activity in this field, Mr. Chambers received the Earl D. Bond Award in June 1965, from the Mental Health Association of Southeastern Pennsylvania.

KENNETH E. APPEL

PREFACE

This book is written for the intelligent layman. I have done my best to avoid the use of technical terms whose precise meanings are known to and used by the trained physician, but which may be meaningless or have incorrect connotations for the lay reader. Though I owe much insight to my psychiatric and psychoanalytic colleagues, I have endeavored to describe symptoms and their cause, and not to use psychiatric or analytical terminology.

The understanding which I have attempted to communicate is based on the study of my own and others' abnormal drinking problems. In this respect, I am most indebted to the late Richard Peabody, a pioneer in helping men and women understand their problems with alcohol, who did a great deal to help me solve my personal drinking problem. In particular, also, I acknowledge my debt to the late Doctor Edward A. Strecker, Professor of Psychiatry, School of Medicine of the University of Pennsylvania, and Consultant and Chief of Service at the Institute of the Pennsylvania Hospital, with whom I collaborated in writing *Alcohol: One Man's Meat* twenty-five years ago. Portions of this book which have stood the test of time are incorporated in the present work.

In 1935, I was given an office at the Institute of the Pennsylvania Hospital in which to carry on my work with men and women who had a problem with alcohol. In 1958, I became a member of the staff. Being a layman, my position was initially difficult and created a great deal of insecurity in

xi

me, but the support of my medical colleagues and the evolution of mutual respect and trust has made my unique position on the staff a rewarding experience.

The term *alcoholic** is not used in this book because it has come to have a nebulous meaning with varying connotations, even among physicians. An addiction to alcohol is not a disease in itself. Instead, it is always a symptom of a given individual's difficulty in making an adequate emotional adjustment to himself and to reality at certain periods in his life. This does not mean that addiction to alcohol as a symptom should be ignored in treatment. Treatment, no matter what approach is being considered, means helping the patient, first, to accept his addiction, second, to deal with the addiction and, third, to understand his own personality which harbored the addiction.

Forty years ago, medicine and psychiatry had a cynical and defeatist attitude toward recovery of the abnormal drinker. I was at that time diagnosed as incurable, which diagnosis, I thank God, was faulty. The "treatment" of that era was in essence an attempt to use persuasion, including threats of premature death or insanity, attempts to shame the patient into a better way of life, and sometimes tear-jerking and sentimental appeals along the line of, "Look what you are doing to those you love and who love you!" Frequently, changes in environment were suggested as therapeutic measures. "Go to Australia or New Zealand, or Africa, and make a new life." Those who followed such advice found that they took their drinking problem right along with them. Sanitariums and mental hospitals were recommended in the vague hope that a period of abstinence might "break the habit."

---

*"The term 'alcoholic problems' is used advisedly in preference to the terms 'alcoholic' and 'alcoholism' which, in our view are stereotyping and over-simplifying, suggesting that all persons with alcohol problems suffer from the same affliction. They do not, except in the sense that drinking alcohol is contra-indicated for them."—*A Position Statement Authorized by the Council of the American Psychiatric Association, February 1965.*

There were in those days new drugs that purported to cure the problem, as there are new drugs today with like promises; but persuasion, shame, threats, changes in environment and drugs have all proved to be ineffectual tools. Such approaches ignore the obvious facts that a man or woman with a drinking problem needs knowledgeable help in order to be able to face it, to understand it, and to overcome it by giving up alcohol permanently.

To face a problem with alcohol along the lines I am indicating demands intelligence and courage. Readaptation of a personality may call for treatment in a hospital or other institution followed by scheduled treatment visits as the patient is learning to accept not-drinking as a way of life. Whether such follow-up treatment demands psychotherapy or deeper psychoanalytic therapy will depend on the individual patient and on the extent and depth of his underlying emotional conflicts. Some patients gain much insight into their underlying conflict through facing and solving their drinking problems while others, much more disturbed, need prolonged courses of psychiatric or analytical help.

It must be obvious that a single rigid, preconceived treatment plan designed to fit all patients will be faulty. Treatment and the extent of it should be based on the understanding of the personality involved. It often takes a long while before a patient knows and trusts the therapist to the point of really sharing his emotional conflicts with him, and it may take many interviews before the patient really agrees to accept help and sees the need for it. Some, on the other hand, ask for help and see the need for treatment in the first interview. Getting a patient to accept treatment by threats or promises or implied guarantee to cure is abhorrent to me. The reverse is much more likely to produce permanent results; namely, convincing the patient that, since the problem lies within him, he and he alone can effect recovery. It is understood that the patient will need much understanding help and will need to share his problems with trained men who are not critical and who take no moral approach toward his addiction.

This approach is a far cry from the "salesmanship" practiced by some. If any salesmanship is involved, it is in the fact that the patient must convince us that he wants treatment and will do his best to share and cooperate in the treatment. It is our duty to tell the patient of the gravity of his illness, but the decision to face his problem and seek help must lie with the patient alone. The patient who makes up his own mind to seek help recovers the first piece of the dignity and self-respect which he lost many years ago. The exception to this approach occurs when we encounter acute alcoholic episodes in which the patient is so confused and out of touch with reality that immediate hospitalization is imperative in order to save him.

This book is dedicated to those who have consulted us over the past thirty-five years. They include some of the finest people I have known, and I owe to them what little knowledge I have gained in this work. Sir William Osler said, "Remember that there is a personality attached to every disease." I will paraphrase this: "Remember that there is a personality attached to every individual's addiction to alcohol." Addiction springs from the personality. We certainly would not get far in helping patients if we ignored this. Twenty-five years ago, I wrote an article for the *Saturday Evening Post* entitled, "The Unhappy Drinker." *Unhappiness* is a relative term, but you may be sure that the personality with a drinking problem suffers from a degree of unhappiness which is incomprehensible to the average man or woman. Our founding fathers in the Declaration of Independence did not guarantee happiness to the citizens of the new nation. They very wisely guaranteed only the right to pursue happiness. Our patients, due to their addiction and the underlying factors which prompt it, are denied the pursuit of happiness in a normal manner. The greatest joy that we experience occurs when we see a patient begin to pursue happiness in a healthy way.

My medical colleagues have urged me to write this book. I have hesitated to do so because it can in no way be considered a scientic treatise on alcoholism. The text is an attempt to convey my feelings about this problem and to show that with certain types of personality with an addiction problem there is hope that it can be solved.

I am not a physician nor a psychiatric specialist, therefore my work with patients has had strict limitations. I am dependent on the internist who, because of his medical training, may save a patient's life with his skill in treating and managing an acute alcoholic episode. I am equally dependent on my psychiatric associates for their diagnostic skill and ability to understand and treat the emotional maladjustments that may underlie the drinking problem. Some of these maladjustments may be so severe that this approach would be futile, and some maladjustments seem to be worked out with the patient's insight into his drinking problem and the cause of it. Relinquishing alcohol as an emotionally sick way of facing life is of necessity a problem of emotional readjustment. My role is, then, a part of a team. The other part of the team is a physician. Any success that I have had is due to the extraordinary support I have always received from my medical colleagues.

FRANCIS T. CHAMBERS, JR.

ACKNOWLEDGMENTS

I would like to express my appreciation to Francis T. Chambers III for his invaluable editing, and to Miss Pearl C. Sickles, my secretary, for the endless hours she gave, typing and retyping the manuscript. I should also like to express my appreciation to a very generous donor who made the writing of this book possible; to the department of Psychiatry of the University of Pennsylvania, which will receive any royalties that accrue from the sale of this book, and to Doctor William L. Peltz for his interest, time and trouble in helping to bring this about. I wish to express my appreciation to the members of the psychiatric staff of the Institute of the Pennsylvania Hospital, who were good enough to read the manuscript and offer me their valuable suggestions.

F. T. C. JR.

CONTENTS

Page

THE DRINKER'S ADDICTION

ADDICTION

Its Nature and
Practical Treatment

Chapter I

THE REGRESSIVE EFFECTS
OF DRINKING ALCOHOL

Backward, turn backward, O Time, in your flight,
Make me a child again, just for to-night! *

As the phenomenon of *regression* plays a very important part in addiction to alcohol and is frequently referred to in the text, it is important that the reader understand the author's definition of the word. There are regressive tendencies in all human beings. For the most part, we indulge these tendencies and frequently get pleasure out of them. When this is the case, we are fortunate in knowing how to handle our regressive tendencies in a non-emotionally-sick way. When I speak of *regression* in this book, I am referring to a very sick form of regression that is incapacitating and will eventually destroy the abnormal drinker if he persists in drinking.

The terms *maturity* and *immaturity* should be thought of with like flexibility, because no adult is completely mature

*Rock Me To Sleep, Mother, by ELIZABETH AKERS ALLEN.

3

and, except in the case of grave mental illness, no adult is completely immature. Maturity is not all white, nor is immaturity all black. The ideal lies in the gray area between the two. In my definition, maturity is an individual's capacity to deal with his immaturity in a non-emotionally-sick way. Regression, as I use it here, refers to the situation where a drinker finds alcohol giving him access to immature levels of behavior normally denied him.

Because alcohol has the extraordinary power of enabling an individual under its influence to go backward in time and to recapture feelings that he experienced prior to becoming an adult, I call its effect *regressive*. There is nothing wrong with the mild regression that takes place in moderate drinking. For those fortunate enough to be able to accept its moderate regressive effect and who have no need to indulge to excess, it is a comfortable adjunct to social occasions. The moderate user of alcohol is permitted a fractional escape from subjective burdens. Perhaps, on a festive occasion, the normal drinker may indulge a little more and recapture a pleasant state of mind which he had as a young adult; or he may even, with a little deeper intoxication, recapture a rather childlike state of mind.

The important thing to realize is that the moderate drinker is in control of his drinking. He calls the regressive shots which permit him a degree of regression pleasant to him and socially approved by those in his environment who are calling their own regressive shots. There is nothing new about this. Devotees of the liquid magic brought about by alcoholic intoxication have existed since before the dawn of history. Sir James George Frazer in his monumental *The New Golden Bough,** speaks of the god of wine as follows:

> The god Dionysus or Bacchus is best known to us as a personification of the vine and of the exhilaration produced by

The New Golden Bough, by SIR JAMES GEORGE FRAZER, New York, Criterion Books, 1959.

the juice of the grape. His ecstatic worship, characterised by wild dances, thrilling music, and tipsy excess, appears to have originated among the rude tribes of Thrace, who were notoriously addicted to drunkenness. Its mystic doctrines and extravagant rites were essentially foreign to the clear intelligence and sober temperament of the Greek race. Yet appealing as it did to that love of mystery and that proneness to revert to savagery which seem to be innate in most men, the religion spread like wildfire through Greece until the god whom Homer hardly deigned to notice had become the most popular figure of the pantheon. The resemblance which his story and his ceremonies present to those of Osiris have led some enquirers both in ancient and modern times to hold that Dionysus was merely a disguised Osiris, imported directly from Egypt into Greece. But the great preponderance of evidence points to his Thracian origin, and the similarity of the two worships is sufficiently explained by the similarity of the ideas and customs on which they were founded.

Frazer points out that Dionysus was able to change himself into various shapes. As a lion, he symbolized strength; as a horse, speed; as a serpent, cunning; and as a bull, potency. We, with the snobbishness of a few thousand years' added civilization, view the mythology of Dionysus with amusement, and yet, in our so-called civilized way, we project onto alcohol today much of the power that the ancients projected onto the god Dionysus. We can note this in mild, and not-so-mild intoxication. For instance, the man with a few too many drinks fancies himself endowed with the strength of a lion, the speed of a horse, the wisdom of the serpent, and the potency of a bull. The tired-eared bartender can bear witness to the drinkers' self-identification with Dionysus. The mystic power of alcohol is revealed in the suggestion that one take a cooling drink of alcohol when hot, and a warming drink of alcohol when cold. Truly, there is something magical about a fluid that cools when you wish it, and heats when you wish it. We can say that Bacchus is still being worshipped by today's drinker, albeit not consciously, as he makes of alcohol the cure-all for many of his emotional difficulties.

Henderson and Gillespie's Textbook of Psychiatry * points out: "It is generally agreed that alcohol is a depressant and not a stimulant, from the very beginning of its direct action on the central nervous system; and that it reduces both mental and muscular efficiency. The deceptive early appearance of stimulation, and the euphoria which misleads the subject into a too favourable view of his performance after he has taken alcohol, arise from the release of the lower nervous centres from control by the higher, by depression of the functions of the latter." This scientific judgment gives us a clue to the almost universal popularity of the narcotic intoxicant, alcohol. It permits us to escape our worries and our tensions, and uninhibits us from our adjustment to civilized standards.

Those fortunate enough to be able to use alcohol in moderation are quite content to limit their regression for the simple reason that they like the adjustment that they have made to reality and feel comfortable in it. No one is always comfortable, but again, a well-adjusted person is willing to meet and face discomfort and to try to solve it. Therefore, the normal social drinker really does not deserve any credit for being a normal social drinker. Since he is well-adjusted to reality and himself, there is no incentive for him, consciously or unconsciously, to seek out deeper levels of intoxication in order to become more comfortable.

Four decades ago, Professor McDougall in his book, *Outline of Abnormal Psychology,* * emphasized the very understandable and strong human incentive for the use of

---

Henderson and Gillespie's Textbook of Psychiatry, 9th ed. Revised by Sir David Henderson and Ivor R. C. Batchelor. London, Oxford, U.P., 1962, p. 51.

Outline of Abnormal Psychology, by WILLIAM MCDOUGALL. New York, Scribner, 1926.

alcohol in a chapter entitled, "Blunting of Self-criticism by Alcohol." The following is his important contribution to the understanding of the intoxication impulse.

Now, of all the intellectual functions, that of self-criticism is the highest and latest developed, for in it are combined the functions of critical judgment and of self-consciousness, that self-knowledge which is essential to the supreme activity we call volition or the deliberative will. It is the blunting of this critical side of self-awareness by alcohol, and the consequent setting free of the emotions and their instinctive impulses from its habitual control, that give the convivial drinker the aspect and the reality of a general excitement.

In the mature, well-developed mind the interplay of thought and emotion goes on under the checking and moderating influence of self-criticism; in social intercourse, especially, it is constantly checked by the thought of the figure one cuts in the eyes of one's fellow men. In proportion, then, as alcohol hampers this process of self-control, the liberation of intellectual or emotional effects goes on at a higher rate. Normally, the emotional states of anxiety, care, and despondency are maintained by self-consciousness, by the repeated turning of the stream of thought to the self, its difficulties, its embarrassments, the snares and dangers that beset its course on every hand, and which are far more frequently imagined and foreseen than actually encountered. Hence, when imaginative self-consciousness is dimmed, the emotions of this class are proportionately less liable to be touched to life, and in the absence of their restraining influence, the other emotions run riot the more gaily.

We now have at least an elementary understanding of just what a man is attempting to do, more or less unconsciously, of course, when he indulges in a glass of beer, a cocktail, or a Scotch and soda. Generally speaking, we may say that alcohol is utilized as an escape from the responsibility and burden of mature emotional life and its decisions. The impulse, then, is regressional. It is an abandonment of emotional maturity. Even the highest degrees of knowledge and maturity fail to withstand the regressive influence of deep intoxication.

Studies of the various phases of emotional development reveal that the capacity for self-criticism does not appear in the individual until adolescence. The teen-ager seems to fluctuate between taking on self-criticism at one moment, and rejecting it at another moment. Likewise, he may fluctuate between a need to be dependent on the parents at one moment, and at another moment, be scornfully aloof of their ignorance and lack of understanding of him.

The abnormal drinker often presents an adolescent fluctuation in mal-dealing with his self-critical faculty. He drinks, which enables him to escape self-criticism. He stops drinking, and is overwhelmed by his self-criticism, at which his only escape seems to be reindulgence in alcohol where he is permitted a regression to a childlike escape from his self-criticism. We might compare the normal, controlled drinker to the abnormal drinker somewhat as follows:

Think of the normal drinker as an executive. He has on his desk a series of buttons which he can press. Button #1 summons his secretary; button #2, the foreman; button #3, the accounting department. The normal drinker has a like system at his disposal in regard to the voluntary control of his drinking. Let us say he presses button #1 by taking two drinks, and this summons a slight escape from fatigue. He presses button #2 with several drinks more, and thus he summons escape from some of his subjective burdens. He presses button #3, which perhaps he reserves for festive occasions, and acquires a mild bun, and incidentally, he may summon the accounting department in the guise of his wife.

The abnormal drinker, on the other hand, has the same series of buttons with the same labels. Before he developed an addictive response to alcohol, he, too, was able to press like buttons with like responses, but since he has developed an abnormal drinking problem the wiring has been changed, and pressing any button that previously permitted controlled, mild regression now results in alarming regression. The patient who is recovering at long last accepts the fact that a change has taken place, and the buttons must be relabeled: *Danger, do not touch.* Much of the resistance to recovery lies in this area.

Let us take, for example, a man who is in charge of his own switchboard, a normal drinker. He is tired and worried because he has had a hard day. It is difficult for him to forget the burdens of an active, competitive existence. He resorts to moderate indulgence in alcohol after a very difficult day at the office. The resulting reaction produces a certain amount of freedom from tenseness and enables him to enjoy the now less-exacting environment. On the other hand, suppose that this man is unknowingly an abnormal drinker. His intention is to indulge for the same reasons that the normal drinker does. The response of the abnormal drinker's promise to himself that he only wants to drink in moderation is belied by the subsequent reaction which demands more and more alcohol. In him we observe, after the relaxing stage, the anesthetic effect of alcohol continually releasing more inhibitions. Self-restraint is thrown to the winds, and occasionally we find intoxicated individuals regressing to infantile behavior or even falling to the level of very primitive reactions.

Fortunately for the individual and for society, in most cases of deep intoxication the narcotic effect of alcohol performs a double service in releasing inhibitions on the one hand, but narcotizing or at least diminishing the force of the resulting action on the other hand. One might say that the fascination of the narcotic effects of alcohol lies in the transitional period between the belief that we can lift ourselves up by our own boot straps, and becoming so narcotized that we never reach the point of making the attempt. The uninhibited mind, freed of its checks and balances by alcohol, fancies itself able to accomplish anything, just before the "passing out" of complete anesthesia destroys all conscious thought.

Studies of the emotions of an infant have revealed that the infant feels for a brief time during his development that he is all-powerful and controlling. This omnipotent feeling also exists for a brief time in deep intoxication.

In moderate indulgence, the reaction is unquestionably pleasant to the majority and consists of feelings of well-being and a self-complimentary state of mind. Fatigue is less noticeable, and the mind is diverted from the worries and annoyances of an exacting business or profession. The individual appears more carefree and not so bowed-down by his problems. The tranquilizing property of alcohol has been recognized for many hundreds of years. By increasing the dose, before it has had a chance to be burned up and eliminated, the drinker experiences the effects of a richer mixture of blood and alcohol being pumped to his brain, and his mental reactions and subsequent behavior become increasingly abnormal. Self-critical faculties become less sharp, normal responsibilities are shirked, and the inhibiting or checking faculties become markedly inactive. Opinions, thoughts, likes and dislikes that normally and sensibly would be left unuttered may now be freely expressed without restraint.

As alcohol mounts in percentage in the blood stream, it begins to influence the lower nervous centers of the brain, and the intoxicated individual becomes thick of speech, slow of movement, and unable to execute coordinated motions. As the influence increases, the nervous centers controlling even the most elementary acts are deadened to such a degree that the man is unable to walk or execute any movement without a paralytic clumsiness. Alcohol has impaired the connection between the brain and the arms and legs. The individual is also emotionally out of control. He may shout and weep or laugh uncontrollably; he may exhibit a recklessness that ends in self-destruction. If, finally, he becomes completely anesthetized by alcohol, he may enter a state of delirium during which he babbles incoherently and makes spasmodic movements like the jerkings and twitchings of an epileptic convulsion. In the last stages, there is a deep anesthesia like that seen in the operating room after ether has been administered.

Prior to the discovery of anesthetics, the practice of getting a patient "dead drunk" before amputations was not uncommon. Here alcohol was being used with the frank understanding of its pain-killing properties. The patient with a drinking problem has made a like discovery. He is using alcohol as an anesthetic, not to deaden physical pain, but to deaden the pain of his personality maladjustment.

To view the panorama of the various stages of intoxication and drunkenness is to witness a progressive psychological descent or regression. The individual is enacting the alcoholic drama of escaping the burdens of maturity, and he may be observed retreating step by step to childish emotional levels. When a certain drunken level is reached, he begins to simulate the reactions of a several months' old infant. If we accept the hypothesis that the results arrived at by drinking are various stages of regression, then we conclude that the incentive that causes one to drink is the unconscious desire to regress. Even the most moderate users of alcohol, who would probably be resentful at having their drinking interpreted as giving rein to a regressive impulse, nevertheless are in search of a fractional amount of release from the surveillance of their mature, self-critical faculties.

At those gay and festive occasions where alcohol flows freely, there is little difficulty in picking out the regressive reactions to alcohol which stimulate its universal popularity. The portly business man of fifty-five tries to act like the young buck of twenty-five. The dowager forgets for a moment the steadying effect of fifty excess pounds and her grown children, and in her alcoholic thoughts and behavior attempts to play the part of the gay and dashing debutante of

thirty years ago. Because the use of alcohol is so generally
socially accepted, many abuse it without fully realizing that
they are treading dangerous ground. For instance, we know
men and women who several nights a week imbibe sufficient
alcohol to produce reactions that show that the lower
nervous centers of the brain are affected. In other words,
they get noticeably "tight." However, their indulgence is
usually restrained to light intoxication involving only the
peak of their self-critical faculties, but on a holiday or
Saturday night they will often imbibe enough alcohol to
permit uncontrollable behavior, totally foreign to their sober
selves. While moderately intoxicated behavior at the present
time is socially accepted in most groups, and quite deep
intoxication is condoned on certain occasions such as
reunions, conventions, etc., the conduct incident to the
presence of enough alcohol to cause the delirium of drunkenness is not welcomed by more sober companions.

Let us consider for a moment those who think of themselves as controlled, moderate drinkers, and yet frequently
drink enough alcohol to become recognizably intoxicated,
though, in no manner of speaking, drunken. These individuals
have acquired a not uncommon technique in self-deception.
Positively and constantly they reiterate, "We can take it or
leave it alone." But can they? Experience teaches that they
seldom "leave it alone" unless there is a very strong incentive
for doing so, in spite of the fact that they often suffer from
decreased efficiency and increasing mental and physical
deterioration, which more abstemious conduct would have
prevented. However, because the norm of drinking is fixed by
social rather than by medical or psychological standards, and
varies from one generation to another, this group is generally
considered the acceptable, controlled users of alcohol of our
time.

In summing up the reasons for the use of alcoholic beverages, it is safe to say that the impulse is not mainly physical,

but psychological or mental. There are, of course, individuals—self-styled gourmets—who claim that the impulse is entirely due to the congenial reaction on their taste buds, and there are others who attribute an improvement in health to the use of alcohol because of its food value;* yet the majority of drinkers are quite willing to admit that were it not for the pleasurable state of mind created by drinking alcohol, they would save their money for other uses. I believe that the majority of drinkers use alcohol to counteract the little annoyances and irritants of life. To the painfully shy, moderate indulgence in alcohol offers relief. Those with fleeting feelings of inferiority (this includes most normal men) find that alcohol will often veneer this distressing reaction to life. A feeling of insecurity can often be banished by a few drinks. In fact, all of the distressing subjective responses to a competitive social environment can be temporarily softened and made more bearable by moderate indulgence in alcohol. We look for and find in alcohol a short vacation from the inhibitions that have been built up throughout the period of evolutionary progression. Man, by the toxic narcotic effect of alcohol on his mind, is permitted to regress by an easy and more or less socially acceptable method.

I do not mean to imply that alcohol is the only instrument of regression. One has only to look around in order to see the same end result achieved by thousands of individuals by means of tantrums, systematized evasions, sympathy

---

*"It is well to repeat that alcohol burned with energy production in the body serves a harmless purpose under certain conditions of moderation of dosage, dilution of form, and ingestion with food, especially for persons engaged in vigorous physical exertion. This limited food value, however, cannot be accepted as a good reason for an individual's taking alcohol, because of the offsetting disadvantages of the drug action of alcohol as a depressant, a narcotic, and, where large amounts are used, a poison, the effects of which continue as long as alcohol remains unburned in the blood." From *Alcohol—Its Effects on Man,* by HAVEN EMERSON, M.D. New York and London, D. Appleton-Century Company, 1934, pp. 26, 27.

hunting, self-pity, and numerous other infantile reality dodging devices. The more serious manifestations of regression are to be found in insanity, the psychoneuroses and drug addiction.

While alcohol is not the only instrument of narcotic regression, it is the only one that may be inexpensively and legally purchased without a doctor's prescription. Perhaps this is why it is almost universally used by people at every economic, social and cultural level. This alone is sufficient reason for more careful scrutiny and more intelligent understanding of the problems produced by alcohol.

The use of alcohol as a social lubricant is a fact of present-day life. This book is not about alcohol nor about the effects of its use in moderation. It is not about a miraculous cure or foolproof treatment for all abnormal drinkers. It is about the problem of the emotionally maladjusted personality who finds in the misuse of alcohol a means to regress to a stage of immaturity. The fact that the misuse and the motivations for that misuse are not understood, and therefore are not consciously faced by the abnormal drinker, gives us a clue to further understanding of his problem and indicates approaches and ways to help the patient try to solve it.

Over my desk passes much literature with catchy titles such as, "Alcoholics are Sick People," "Alcoholics Need Help," "Alcoholics Can Be Cured." What is meant by "alcoholics are sick people"? If they are sick, why are they sick? Does "sick" mean a physical illness or an emotional illness, or does it mean both? I agree with the statement, "Alcoholics need help," but the important question is, what kind of help is a given individual going to respond to? The statement, "Alcoholics can be cured" is obviously false because many an individual with an addiction to alcohol has proved resistant to any approach or treatment. The word "cure" may mean arresting an addiction by means of administering a drug that makes the patient violently ill if he drinks, or it may mean that he becomes a dedicated member of Alcoholics Anonymous and this enables him to stop drinking; or it may mean that he has to understand himself and the structure of his addiction problem as well as the underlying personality that turned to alcohol. Thirty-five years of constant contact with personalities with drinking problems have humbled me a great deal. I must admit I do not know what an alcoholic is. *Alcoholic* is nothing but a label. I use the terms *abnormal drinker* and *addict* because to me they mean a divergence from normal, no more and no less.

The next logical challenge to those of us who are trying to understand the problem is, Why is drinking abnormal in certain individuals? We find the patient does not know, and I certainly do not know, having just met the patient. Treatment then begins as a mutual exploration of cause and effect, and is free of prejudgment and diagnostic labels or generalizations such as, "The alcoholic is . . . ." As I bring out later, each patient is a separate research project because no two personalities are identical. As in internal medicine, diagnosing the disease is not enough. The physician is not satisfied until he understands the disease and what caused it, at which time he has a better chance to treat it effectively. In this chapter I have tried to convey that there are unconscious regressive needs that the patient is blindly searching for, and that he finds a temporary fulfillment of these needs in intoxication.

Alcohol addiction indicates a progressive need to regress and this leads me to the conclusion that the regressive needs we defended ourselves against in forming our personalities are crumbling under the sway of alcohol addiction. Acceptance of the fact that alcohol can and does give us an access to regression brings us closer to understanding one facet of this problem: you cannot produce identical symptoms except through the regressive reaction to alcohol. This reaction may be very like other regressive symptoms encountered in mental illness and the causative factors may be very similar, but let us not lose sight of the uniqueness of addiction to alcohol; namely, you have to drink alcohol in order to obtain alcohol-ically-induced regression. No other drug, no mental illness, has identical behavioral symptoms.

In further chapters, I hope to show at least theoretically some of the maladjustments of personality that may culminate in addiction to alcohol, as well as some of the reasons these pre-drinking maladjustments occur. As the material on treatment is based on the understanding of the problem described in previous chapters, the dynamics of treatment are influenced by the evaluation of each personality who consults us. I use the term "dynamics of treatment" as it indicates the purpose of a therapy which is to show the patient the motion of his maladjustment and help him understand the causative factors in producing it.

A like interpretation can be given to the word *static*. We might say that static treatment is treatment in which the emphasis is put on arresting the addiction without searching for the source. The purpose of this book is to show that treatment is directed at changing the motion of maladjustment. If the forces that caused a man to become addicted are understood and redirected into constructive channels, we can see that these forces were not at fault, but the patient's blind application of these forces placed him on a collision course with destruction.

Chapter II

WHO HAS AN ADDICTION
PROBLEM WITH ALCOHOL?

Drinking and its reaction on the behavior of men and women differs with each person who uses it. Alcohol is used because people like its effect. The use of alcoholic beverages has become part of social life in a large segment of our society. When used in moderation alcohol is a pleasant social lubricant. Most people use it in various degrees of moderation, but all people who drink are to some degree dependent on alcohol. For instance, if they are accustomed to drinking at certain times, they would miss it if it were denied them at these times, but again, if this dependency is moderate, it does not constitute a problem. The appeal of alcohol lies in a number of pleasurable responses to its effect. One of these is its power to blunt our self-critical faculties. It also anesthetizes the senses that make us feel fatigued, which fact explains the common but incorrect assumption that alcohol is a stimulant. As pointed out previously, alcohol is scientifically accepted as a depressant. It also has a tranquilizing effect, and permits many people to forget their subjective burdens temporarily.

It is obvious that drinking is interwoven with much of our

17

social life. The wedding, cocktail party, or any festive occasion calls for drinking. The golf or tennis game is followed by cooling drinks in the club house. To ask a man or a woman to have a drink with you is a gesture of friendliness. We are bombarded by advertisements for whiskies, wines and beers. These advertisements bear the implication that we cannot really play without alcohol. They imply that a vacation would fall flat without this or that brand which they are advertising. The distinguished-looking man is photographed drinking his favorite brand. Again, the implication is that he is successful and distinguished because he drinks a certain brand of whiskey. It certainly would not be good advertising to photograph the distinguished-looking man on a stretcher being taken to a hospital because he had become too dependent on this or that brand of whiskey.

The appeal of alcohol to its users is emphasized by the fact that our citizens pay very high taxes each year for the privilege of its use, and pay tremendous sums to satisfy their dependency on it. I quote a southern senator's amusing speech because it is pretty much the way most people think of the problem:

> You have asked me how I feel about whisky. All right, here is just how I stand on this question:
>
> If, when you say whisky, you mean the devil's brew, the poison scourge, the bloody monster that defiles innocence, yea, literally takes the bread from the mouths of little children; if you mean the evil drink that topples the Christian man and woman from the pinnacles of righteous, gracious living into the bottomless pit of degradation and despair, shame and helplessness and hopelessness, then certainly I am against it with all of my power.
>
> But, if when you say whisky, you mean the oil of conversation, the philosophic wine, the stuff that is consumed when good fellows get together, that puts a song in their hearts and laughter on their lips and the warm glow of contentment in their eyes; if you mean Christmas cheer; if you mean the stimulating drink that puts the spring in the old gentleman's step on a frosty

morning; if you mean the drink that enables a man to magnify his joy, and his happiness, and to forget, if only for a little while, life's great tragedies and heartbreaks and sorrows, if you mean that drink, the sale of which pours into our treasuries untold millions of dollars, which are used to provide tender care for our little crippled children, our blind, our deaf, our dumb, our pitiful aged and infirm, to build highways, hospitals and schools, then certainly I am in favor of it.

This is my stand. I will not retreat from it; I will not compromise.*

Out of an adult population of approximately one hundred and twelve million, it is estimated that five million have an addiction problem with their drinking. (I can find no exact scientific basis for this figure; therefore it must be accepted only as a rough estimate.) By addiction to alcohol, I mean that their manner of drinking is incapacitating certain individuals in their work, their marriages and their relationships with their fellow human beings. These estimated five million abnormal drinkers pose a tremendous economic problem in lost man-hours and in the cost of state or private hospitalization, not to mention the relief that must be sought by many of their dependents, as well as the damage done to the mental health of these families. Parents with severe drinking problems spawn disturbed children who are liable to be afflicted with mental illness or delinquency, and these children in turn will need help in child guidance clinics, and often hospitalization or custodial care. Taking all these factors into consideration, the expense involved in the estimated five million abnormal drinkers is astronomical.

I am sure that no one wants to add himself to the large number of addictive drinkers who exist today. Therefore, it is important to differentiate between those who use alcohol with no serious consequences, and those whose use of it is destroying them. Unfortunately, it is very easy and very dangerous to think in black and white terms. The man having

*From *The Wall Street Journal,* Dow Jones & Company, Inc., December 23, 1965.

a pleasant drink in a cocktail lounge while he flirts with his best girl, or the tired businessman who welcomes a cocktail or two with his wife before dinner seem poles apart from the poor wretch strapped to a stretcher, screaming with fear at the threatening hallucinations of his delirium tremens. These examples do not seem to jibe, but it may well be that the man with the d.t.'s was having a pleasant drink with his best girl or several cocktails with his wife ten or fifteen years ago, and at that time had no fears that he would end up in an acute alcoholic episode such as I have described.

The point I wish to make is that addiction to alcohol is often an insidious and gradually creeping dependency on alcohol that can go unrecognized by the man or woman involved and by those who are close to them. How then do we spot this creeping abnormal dependency on alcohol in ourselves and those close to us?

In reviewing the history of their drinking, patients often reveal that their intake of alcohol was becoming progressively greater but that, with the technique of rationalization, they had in the past been able to disguise from themselves and their husbands or wives that their dependency on alcohol had become an addiction. The technique of rationalization is probably used at times by all of us in our attempts to save our self-respect. It is a very common form of not facing ourselves, and is by no means unique to the abnormal drinker. In the early phases of abnormal drinking, we see it used in the following way. A man may say to his wife, "I had everything go wrong in the office today. I need a few extra drinks." This may be an isolated incident, and of no importance, but if the extra drinks are demanding more and more rationalization, this in itself may herald an increasing dependency on alcohol.

We see rationalization unrelated to alcohol as, for instance, in a man who cannot hold a job for long. He rationalizes as follows: "It must be my boss' fault, he's such an s.o.b." By this technique he is able to avoid facing his lack of skill or his inefficiency. He saves face to himself, but seldom fools his associates. In Chapter VI, I will discuss the rationalizing process in detail, as it plays so prominent a part in addiction to alcohol.

Another early tendency is the habit of slipping oneself extra drinks while mixing them for guests; or the need to stop on the way home to establish the foundation for future drinking at home. In the early stages of addiction, people are apt to get a little touchy about their drinking and become self-conscious about it. Soon defensive lying may well become a part of it. For instance, "I just had one beer at the club before I came home," may mean that the speaker actually has had a good many drinks. Another significant habit is lone drinking, rather than social drinking. This seems to be a symptom of addiction. The underlying difference seems to be covered by a recent patient who remarked, "I have for many years wanted a drink before dinner or at social occasions, but now I seem to need it more and more, unrelated to social occasions."

A rather brusque industrialist consulted me some years ago. Challengingly, he demanded that I give him one sound reason why he could not drink in moderation. My reply was, "Because you don't want to drink in moderation." After some time and valiant experiments to prove I was wrong, he did return for treatment and was able to admit to himself that if he drank, moderate drinking was not enough for him. The decision of the patient to accept this fact is one of his most difficult decisions, because in all probability he has been through a stage of moderate drinking, or at least a stage of nonaddictive drinking earlier in his life. He reasons: "I most certainly don't want to become a drunkard. Therefore, I will use my willpower and drink in moderation." Such reasoning lacks the understanding that he needs so badly, the understanding that a deep addiction dependency on alcohol now exists in him and that the return to drinking anything will reexcite this addiction.

Here are three questions that I think I should try to answer: First, Can the onset of addiction be prevented? Second, Can abnormal drinking be arrested and social drinking indulged in? Third, When has the borderline from carefree, social drinking been crossed into a deep, slavish addiction?

To answer the first: One thing we have learned through experience is that the Nineteenth Amendment was a great failure. We proved then that you cannot legislate against addiction. We believe that abnormal drinking is a maladjustment in a given personality starting far back in the formative years of the child. The answer then to the question, Can abnormal drinking be prevented? is, Yes, if the child has well-adjusted parents, aware of the responsibilities of sharing the growth struggle of their child, and understanding the problems of engendering mental health in themselves and their offspring.

I once suggested to one of my colleagues that he write a book with the title, "Children with Growing Parents." I meant, of course, the emotional development and understanding of the parent role. Today, in high school, biological knowledge of sex may be gained. The moral responsibilities of sex may be absorbed from parents, teachers and church, but the responsibility of marriage and bringing up children is still largely left to instinct and guesswork. Instinct and guesswork are not enough in this complex industrialized world of today. My hope is that we will soon start teaching children at school to understand their very important role in bringing up future children to obtain mental health and maturity. I feel that such teaching would enable future mothers and fathers to help their children avoid maladjustments that can lead to addiction to alcohol or mental illness.

The second question was, Can abnormal drinking be arrested and social drinking be indulged in? The word *abnormal* must be defined before this is answered, since the word has many connotations. There are certainly men and women who decide that they are drinking excessively and curtail this drinking because of that realization. There are men and women who reveal normally hidden personality traits when they drink, and would do well not to use alcohol for this reason alone. For instance, we have the person who becomes belligerent or obscene or boastful and whose behavior embarrasses his companions. These revelations may or may not be forerunners of an addiction problem, but once drinking has reached a stage where it is a necessary crutch to the personality so that the drinker finds he is addicted to alcohol, I have found that the only possible way he can readjust his life is to relinquish alcohol completely, and to do this demands a good deal of self-understanding and outside help.

My answer to the second question, Can addiction be arrested and social drinking indulged in? is No. This "no" is based on thirty-five years of work—in conjunction with some of the outstanding psychiatrists of our day—with men and women who were addicted to alcohol.

The answer to the third question, When has the borderline from carefree social drinking been crossed into a deep, slavish dependency known as addiction? is not so easy to arrive at because addictive drinking is so frequently an insidious, progressive dependency. We could compare it to crossing the border from the State of Maine into Canada. Were it not for the Customs inspectors at the border, it would be very difficult to know when you had passed that border. The nearest I can come to a clear-cut answer to this question is, when a man or woman's life, liberty and pursuit of happiness are interfered with by their manner of drinking, and they persist in drinking and find they cannot stop in spite of the addiction threat to their total personality, then their drinking is a problem. It is a problem, though, that can often be solved if the patient has the courage and the tenacity to seek help in order to solve it. One encouraging factor I have noticed over many years of working in this field is that society and patients themselves, due to much discussion of the problem in newspapers and magazines, are beginning to recognize it as a form of maladjustment for which treatment is available.

In the early days of the Roman Empire, there was a saying, *in vino veritas*—"in wine, the truth"; and in the first century A.D., Seneca, a philosopher of great repute, made the observation that intoxication was self-induced insanity.

Let us for a moment discuss these interesting observations made so many hundreds of years ago. To my delight, I recently heard a modern version of these ancient observations. It was part of a conversation between two women in a restaurant in Europe. They had, perhaps, had one too many cocktails. One turned to the other and said, "My dear, after the fourth cocktail your personality starts showing just a little too much." The thing that interests me is that all three observations, the two ancient ones and the very modern one, have a great deal of truth in them.

There is no doubt, even to the casual observer, that alcohol has the effect of blunting our faculty of self-criticism. Most personalities contain a standard of what that individual personality feels it should be like, and this standard, to various degrees, requires suppression of a part of us that would be incompatible with it. Very often, after a few too many drinks, the self-critical faculties are narcotized by alcohol, and the personality reveals normally suppressed tendencies in itself. We have probably all observed this in others and, perhaps, in ourselves. I do not mean to imply that there is anything wrong in this. A few examples of this very common phenomenon may help to clarify what I mean.

The past-middle-aged lady with grown children and grand-children may become flirtatious and think of herself as the dashing belle of eighteen that she was many, many years ago.

The one-time hot shot on the campus may talk interminably about the days when he was the captain of the football team in college, or the man who has had war experience may, after a few too many drinks, immediately start bringing up that exciting and dramatic period of his life.

Such things are very mild and do nobody any great harm. But then we get into a little more serious revelation of the inner personality which sometimes is exhibited under the influence of alcohol, such as a degree of excessive exhibitionism in women who normally are quite modest, or sexual promiscuity, when the self-critical faculties which would be normally inhibited in sobriety, are anesthetized. Sometimes husbands and wives who have a sadomasochistic relationship (where one of them has a need to be punished, and the other a need to punish) will reveal this under the influence of alcohol to the embarrassment and distress of their more sober friends. Such relationships do exist, but in sobriety they are usually kept under cover, and though they may be normally exercised only in the intimacy of the home, they will come out and reveal themselves with even a slight degree of intoxication.

There seems to exist in this highly competitive society, a far-too-prevalent custom of wife and husband after a hard day's work slugging themselves with a good many drinks in the intimacy of the home. The tragedy of this is that they exclude their children. A younger patient expressed this to me rather well in one of our conferences. He said, "My father and mother were by no means drunkards, but when we were children, we always knew that after a few drinks we were no longer part of the family group. Mother and Father seemed to leave us."

There is another quite common characteristic exhibited by those in advanced years who have been normal social drinkers for a large part of their adult life, perhaps with a fairly heavy intake of alcohol, but in no way to be considered abnormal. When they reach the age of fifty-five, sixty, or sixty-five, the same amount of alcohol that they could tolerate earlier now has an adverse effect on them. The number of drinks that they used to tolerate so well is now too much, and it becomes more obvious. Their speech becomes slurred, and they are apt to tell a story and then repeat it to the same audience an hour or two later. Again, there is no great harm in this, but it would be wise for men and women after the age of fifty to realize that their tolerance to alcohol is decreasing, and that the curtailing of their intake will probably add to their own enjoyment and the enjoyment of those who love them.

I hope that the reader will not get the impression that I have a Carrie Nation complex or think that all drinking is evil and that banishing alcohol from our lives would be the solution for all the distress, poverty and troubles of the world. I do not believe this. I think that for those who have no problem with alcohol it is a pleasant social aid to conviviality, and that for the minority, which includes myself, it is absolutely poisonous both physiologically and psychologically, because in this minority the use of it happens to be a psychologically sick way of facing life.

Some years ago, I was consulted by a very able and intelligent Jew. When I got to know him better, I remarked to him one day how rare it was that I had had patients of his faith, and asked him if he could give me an explanation of this. His reply, whether it is the right or wrong answer, is interesting. He said, "We, as a people, have been persecuted for so many hundreds of years that we instinctively don't want to lose ourselves in intoxication because we realize that then we are more vulnerable." I think society en masse could take its cue from this remark. In essence, it means that moderate drinking is common sense in all professions, careers, the diplomatic field, the army, the navy and the sciences.

It may be very exciting to read the gossip columnists' accounts of the actions of the playboys and playgirls in cafe society, and of the movie queens and their consorts for whom publicity, even adverse publicity, seems to be their life's blood. But by and large, if you analyze them, many of these are men and women who never grew up and are still acting out an adolescent phase of growth. This group has never learned that you cannot buy happiness, and when one ends up in a sanitarium or hospital or under psychiatric care, as many of them do, he soon learns that he cannot buy recovery, either. Recovery, if it is to take place, means a tremendous effort on the patient's part to understand his regression needs plus a long, hard job readjusting and readapting his personality.

Chapter III

SOME SYMPTOMS OF
HAVING AN ADDICTION TO ALCOHOL

Many addicted drinkers have the same predisposing factors that are found in symptoms of mental illness. Why one person seeks escape in alcohol and not in manifestations of mental illness, we do not know.

Unhappily, one still encounters, even among intelligent people, adherents to the doctrine of predestined or inherited alcoholic damnation, i.e., that because one or more ancestors were drunkards, the offspring must of necessity become addicts. Let me say with all possible emphasis that this is fallacious. Another very common misconception is that a man or woman turns to the bottle because of some distressing and shocking episode in his life. I grant that such an episode may spark the beginning of addiction, but it is my belief that the fuse was already there waiting to be lit by the spark. Let us say that a man fails in business and turns to alcohol. Another man or woman may have an unhappy marriage and turn to alcohol, while a woman may lose a loved husband on whom she was dependent and turn to alcohol. But the vast majority of people at some time in their lives must face shocks, losses, failures, frustrations, or humiliations, and they meet these shocks, face them and go on with their lives without turning to alcohol. I do not mean to imply that men and women who have developed an integrated personality are emotional rocks of Gibraltar. They suffer anguish and great emotional upsets. You cannot get through life without encountering such things. They may not take them very well, but the fact that they take them and do not run away from them means that they have established a workable personality.

I would like to dwell for a minute on Freud's concept that there are life instincts in all of us. They include sex and self-preservation, and I would like to show how the life instinct is drastically interfered with when a person has an addiction problem.

Let us take, first of all, sex. Conflict about sex is first felt in early childhood and reaches a peak in adolescence, and one may expect to have conflict about sex for the balance of life. What role, then, does alcohol play in the sex life of the addicted drinker? One thing we can be sure of is that the addict is not facing and resolving his ever-present conflict about sex. To some degree we observe in the addicted drinker an evasion of mature sexual responsibility. One could say that sex cannot compete with an alcoholic addiction. Deep intoxication renders a man impotent and a woman frigid, and many marriages go on the rocks because the husband or wife of the addicted drinker soon feels frustrated and rejected by a partner who obviously prefers alcohol to sex. It has been my observation that if a person with a drinking problem relinquishes alcohol, with understanding, he or she usually acquires a happier sexual adjustment with wife or husband, though it may take time before this adjustment takes place.

There are, of course, unmarried men and women with an addiction problem who seek sexual gratification in casual love affairs or by having a lover. Usually, the lover is married. I think that this is often the case because while the patient is unconsciously looking for sexual gratification, he or she is at the same time avoiding the mature responsibilities that go with marriage, such as having children and taking care of a family.

We encounter in our work a small proportion of people with an overt homosexual problem. Tragically, many of these patients have married and have had children in a vague, blind hope that marriage might solve their deep emotional maladjustment. Unhappily, this is not the solution for homosexuality. From my observation, I do not believe that the incidence of abnormal drinking is any more or less prevalent in the ranks of homosexuals than elsewhere. I am sorry to say that in my experience with patients, I have seen homosexual patients who were able to relinquish alcohol completely and to adjust their lives without it, but who have been unable to relinquish their homosexual appetites. I have always suggested to them that they seek analytical therapy in order to try to understand and resolve this aspect of their personality problem. With very few exceptions, such patients have refused psychoanalytic treatment.

I think we can safely generalize that the person with a drinking problem is immature sexually, and it often seems as if he was still in the adolescent throes of conflict about sex. In other words, he never outgrew his preadult level with any degree of peace and satisfaction. Up to the time he might seek help in solving his drinking problem, we see a progressive regression. By this I mean that he is unconsciously reaching backward rather than forward to solve his conflict. As I have pointed out, the regression that is normally denied the healthy adult is not denied the person with an addiction problem. You can, in deep intoxication, reach a dependency level equivalent to that of the infant in the crib.

Another aspect of the instinctive drive is the need for man to share and enjoy things with other people and to participate with his fellowman in joint efforts. This can be one of man's most rewarding characteristics. How does addiction interfere with this healthy need? In answering this, we must take into consideration that very often insecure, shy people use alcohol to overcome their shyness in order to feel *en rapport* with the herd; but that if this is carried to an addiction to alcohol, the herd moves away from such an individual, and in all likelihood the individual moves away from the herd. I often encounter lonely, rejected people who do not realize that they themselves have done the rejecting by having an addiction to alcohol.

The self-preservation instinct certainly cannot be fulfilled in a person with a drinking problem, for after all, the patient is destroying himself. Though the patient may be fearful of premature death because of his addiction, I have never seen anyone permanently frightened out of drinking.

Many years ago, I saw a travelogue about how natives in the South Seas captured monkeys. The natives bored a small hole in one end of a coconut. They then stapled a chain to the other end of the coconut, and attached the chain to a tree. Before leaving, they poured some grain into each coconut, and then went off and hid in the brush. After a while the little monkeys came chattering down out of the trees in full view of the telescopic camera lens. They examined the coconuts and found that they could just get one paw into the hole in order to reach the grain, and then they tried with a fist full of grain to pull their paws out of the small hole in the coconut. Because the fist contained the grain, they could not get their paws out. Soon the natives approached with their baskets to capture the monkeys and send them off to civilization. The poor little monkeys, screaming with fear, never relinquished the fist full of grain that might have permitted them to escape. When I saw this travelogue, it reminded me intensely of my own problem with alcohol and of the problems I regularly encounter in those who consult me.

A crude way to explain reeducation is that, through understanding of the patients' problem, we help them to relinquish, finger by finger, their blind, self-destructive grip on alcohol. The analogy may seem so crude that it is not worthy of the intelligent reader's consideration. It nevertheless points out to us that the mechanism that grips the patient with an addiction is just as little understood by him as the mechanism that gripped the little monkeys was understood by them. When I saw this travelogue, I kept thinking, "You little fools, why don't you let go of the grain and scamper up the trees and be happy again and avoid destruction?" Yet at the same time, I realized that the poor little monkeys had not developed the brain capacity to relinquish the food on which they were dependent in order to escape destruction. Fortunately, most addicted drinkers have the brain capacity, but due to emotional blockage they are unable, without treatment, to use it toward relinquishing alcohol. You will notice throughout this book that I have frequently used the phrase "relinquish alcohol," rather than the more popular terms. "Relinquish" connotes that the patient, with insight rather than willpower, does it himself.

The personal peculiarities of the addicted drinker are many and varied, but we can certainly include in them an exaggerated tendency to self-deception and a technique of rationalizing trivial, emotional upsets into reasons for the continuance of drinking or for relapses after treatment is started. Rationalization is such an important element in the psychology of the addicted drinker that it deserves further explanation. We are all familiar with the word camouflage. A lethal gun emplacement is made to look like a shady nook by camouflage. Rationalization is mental camouflage. It changes and disguises a sick response to reality such as addiction. The addict, not realizing the reasons for his abnormal drinking, is looking for a scapegoat, and so he blindly gets into the habit of rationalizing his reasons for drinking. He blames it on the attitude of his wife, or on circumstances, or on things that upset him or things that make him nervous. In fact, he goes through a period of blaming nearly everything for his abnormal drinking, rather than facing the truth which is that he has an addiction to alcohol that he cannot relinquish.

If we look at the problem of addiction objectively, we can see that rationalization is of necessity a dominant motive in the psychology of a person who has a sick dependency on alcohol. As I have pointed out, marital discord as it relates to sex is naturally prevalent in the addicted drinker, but marital discord, as it relates to other aspects of the husband-wife relationship, is also soon called into play to fortify the rationalizing process. Most addicted drinkers suffer feelings of inferiority and insecurity, and we may even find a patient excusing lack of success in life on the grounds that drinking prohibited the potential superman from gaining his natural desserts! Thus, he throws his ego ideal a sop, and gives his addiction increased momentum and psychological importance. As far as the addicts with some ego development are concerned, we have found that they tend to be truthful when sober, but untruthful while drinking, and particularly do they lie to husbands or wives about anything pertaining to their addiction problem. They become progressively unstable as their addiction increases. Depression due to bad news and exaltation due to favorable news seem to be the surface emotional factors that lead to further drinking occasions. They are bored with most phases of life, which is only natural when one takes into consideration the fact that this boredom can be dissipated very quickly by intoxication and drunkenness.

One of my psychoanalytical associates, Dr. G. Henry Katz, stresses that boredom results from an instinctive drive being considerably repressed. Most patients, although not all, present a picture of being attractive and good-natured. They seem to be more dramatic than the average. They express a great need to be liked and loved and thought well of, but they seek to satisfy these very human needs more as children do than as adults do. Nevertheless, eliminating some of the insane and mentally defective addicts, we have every reason to believe that our patients are often intellectually above the average rather than below it, lacking an organization of personality, rather than revealing a permanent defect in personality.

It is very difficult for the addict to accept the fact that he has stepped over the line of social drinking and is now an addicted drinker. Let us take an example of this.

Mr. X has a responsible position, a charming wife, fine children, and apparently everything for which to live. At twenty-eight, he seems to have a bright future ahead of him. He has been drinking a good deal for the past ten years, but he has limited this drinking to stag parties, and to festive occasions when he and his friends let loose on weekends and holidays. His wife has occasionally been worried about him, and has often been ashamed of his behavior because he seemed to get more intoxicated than his friends. However, until recently he has always been able to go to work, and she has not felt that his drinking was a real problem in his life. Lately, though, a subtle change has taken place. His hangovers and depressions after a Saturday or holiday night have become more and more acute, and a tendency not to remember incidents that took place while he was drinking is becoming progressively more apparent. A number of times he has had to have several stiff drinks on the morning after a drinking occasion in order to steady his overwrought nerves, and when he gets home in the evening he is depressed and nervous until he has unlocked the sideboard and poured himself a few drinks. He can hardly wait for the lunch hour when he can escape from the office to get more of the "nerve steadier." Lately he has missed several days at the office because he was afraid that his shaking condition would be criticized. After missing a day, his return to the office is accompanied by a fit of nerves, and he feels that people are talking about his condition. He becomes very sensitive about his drinking, and any casual, jocose remark made by a friend about some drinking occasion is resented.

Such a state of mind may exist for a long while, becoming progressively worse as more alcohol is consumed to combat the initial feelings of shame caused by his behavior on drinking parties. This transitional state is psychologically painful beyond the power of the normal drinker's comprehension. It is a beginning of the disorganization of a personality which has become addicted to alcohol. When this stage is arrived at, self-respect is shattered and is relieved only by drinking. It is interesting that highly intelligent men and women, though they may have a shattering addiction to alcohol which is ruining everything in their lives, can maintain such a resistance against giving in and realizing that their drinking has become an addiction rather than a social use. It is gratifying that in recent years business, industry and the professions have gradually come to accept addiction as a symptom of personality illness. Patients are frequently referred to me from these sources. As the president of a large corporation said to me relative to the man he had referred, "We have a great deal of investment and training in this man. If he can be helped, we want to help him." Sometimes, patients referred from such sources do recognize their problem and seek help in earnest. However, some fifty per cent of them in my experience deny the problem of addiction, and in due course they are fired and this usually accelerates their downhill pace.

It must be obvious that a state of mental conflict in which the individual is resisting the recognition of his complete dependency on alcohol by pretending to himself that his drinking is not important is very destructive to his happiness. All of the self-deceptive mechanisms are brought into play in order to justify a continuance of drinking.

The list of my patients includes business men, scientists,

politicians, the clergy, physicians and occasionally even psychiatric specialists. This must be bewildering to the layman, who says to himself, "The men in medicine, and psychiatrists in particular, must know through their observation of the awful effect of addiction. How can they develop a problem?" They can and do, and the answer is much the same as it is in the layman who develops a problem. He thinks, "It can't happen to me." In many such instances, everybody is aware of what the drinker is doing and, like the ostrich who buries his head in the sand to avoid danger, he is fooling nobody but himself. If the toxic effects of alcohol render medical assistance imperative during this period, the tactful physician can often seize this opportunity to suggest that his patient's drinking is far from social, that it has become an addiction, and that the patient is therefore in need of professional help.

As has been pointed out, it has been proved to all of us who have endeavored to help the addicted drinker that the purely emotional plea, no matter how well expressed, does little more than aggravate the drinking. Lectures and warnings are of little avail, and the temporary measure of going "on the wagon" for stated periods of time never enables the addict to reach a level of drinking in moderation.

As I have told my students, if a man seeks help and does not have conflict about whether or not to drink again, the patient and those who are helping him are in real trouble. Anyone in this field must have observed what is known as the flight into recovery. The patient has had a bad breakdown and is in need of hospitalization. He comes to my office and says, "Mr. Chambers, I have learned my lesson. I am determined never to drink again, and I am leaving to go home and see no necessity for further help."

I am sure that the patients who tell us this really believe what they say, but they are in for inevitable future trouble. These patients do not realize that having conflict and learning how to resolve it is actually part of every man's and woman's mature living. Suppressing conflict, which is actually what the man or woman does in these flights into recovery, merely means that he has put a lid on the conflict for the time being, and that pretty soon the lid will blow off again.

I, personally, when in the throes of an acute alcoholic addiction, had these flights into recovery. I remember a very distressing period during which I had delirium tremens of short duration. When I cleared up, my wife came into the hospital, and I said to her, "Sweetie, you and I never have to worry again about my drinking. I've had it. I've been insane because of my drinking, and the problem is solved." When I said this, I meant it from the bottom of my heart, and yet in three months I was drinking, and I had rationalized it somewhat as follows: "All right, I've had this terrible shock. Now I will drink in moderation. Knowing full well what abnormal drinking did to me, this will act as a crutch to keep my drinking moderate." And so I again started to drink, and in due course found that moderation was completely impossible for me.

Another very common misconception on the part of the patient is that periods of abstinence limited to a certain length of time such as a month, a year, or ten years, will help in solving a drinking problem, for when a self-imposed period of abstinence is over and drinking is reindulged in, usually with the idea that this time it will be moderate, the conflict rapidly reappears, and the drinking does not long remain moderate.

Most patients describe in their histories self-imposed abstinence periods, and the fact that they have tried this compromise and proved that it did not work may be one of the factors that led them to seek deeper understanding of their problem and how to solve it. As we get into the chapter on treatment, the reader will easily see why these self-imposed periods of abstinence accomplish so little toward a permanent personality readjustment. As a rule, in the progressive course of addiction, the periods of sobriety become shorter and shorter until they finally disappear, and then there is the picture of the addict finding in alcohol a continuous compensation for his maladjustment. At this period, he dreads returning to sobriety because it means a return to a state of mind which he finds intolerable. Consequently, he attempts to prolong a toxically created state of mind to the point of oblivion. On awakening from a drugged sleep, reality plus the self-inflicted wound to his ego ideal, caused by his addicted drinking, offer a still greater incentive for escape, and this vicious circle develops into a condition of chronic addiction which may well demand institutional care and treatment before the patient has a chance of facing any phase of reality without alcohol.

Once a man has become addicted to alcohol, we must separate in our conception the problem of his early drinking days and the problem of his later breakdown with alcohol. His initial drinking may have been within social limits, or of a dissipated variety; however, up to the time of its decidedly abnormal manifestations, his personality discomforts were of a nonaddicted nature, and we believe that at this period he depended on alcohol as a form of quasi-adjustment. After his drinking becomes uncontrollable, we get the picture of a man drinking not only to escape the discomfiture of his maladjustment, but also to escape the facing of the regressive outflowing from his unconscious mind. The emergence of primitive feelings into the partially anesthetized conscious mind of the patient are too painful to face, and so he resorts to deeper intoxication.

In all the years that I have had contact with cooperative patients, I have never been able to get any patient to recall the way he felt when deeply intoxicated. The usual reply to my questioning is, "I just blacked out" or "I can't remember." It is my belief that this blacking out is a purposive defense measure because via alcohol access to primitive infantile levels is available. So shocking is this access to the personality involved that repression is automatically applied on gaining the state of sobriety. In observing patients who are deeply intoxicated, it is very easy to see how like their actions are to those of an infant. Here we see a complete narcissistic regression in the intoxicated patient, and one can interpret the state of mind as being, "I am helpless and dependent. I love only me. In this self-love I am safe."

In the past, I have frequently posed this question to residents who admitted deeply intoxicated patients to the hospital: "If this man hadn't alcohol on his breath, and you had no indication that he had been drinking, what would be your snap diagnosis?" The answer has been that they would think the patient was psychotic. When this point has been reached, we can compare the alcoholic impulses stemming from unconscious conflict in the mind of the addict to a radio we have left turned on in a low key while we are studying or writing. As long as we are concentrating, we are not aware of the dim music, but when we pause in our work and relax, rhythm of the music at once becomes evident to us. The addict attempting to overcome his dependency on alcohol has a mental phenomenon very similar to this. When he is concentrating on his work or his hobbies, he is not conscious of the monotonous alcoholic theme song, "Another little drink won't do me any harm."

However, let his concentration lag, and be displaced by detachment or daydreams, and the unconscious radio sends out the destructive impulses to escape conflict by the habitual method, drinking. Perhaps to the reader who is a teetotaler or who has always drunk in moderation, this may all seem to be too fanciful and farfetched. However, after some years of consultation with sincere men and women who are anxious to open up the inner recesses of their minds in order to arrive at a non-alcoholic-dependent solution for their state of mental conflict, I am convinced that the addicted drinker really does not know why he drinks any more than the lady with the nervous breakdown knows why she has fainting spells or palpitations of the heart or many other neurotic symptoms.

When we say that the addict does not know why he drinks except that he is bombarded by impulses to take a drink, we make a statement that is difficult to understand. In order to make this nonreasoning drinking clear, it may be compared to the scientific phenomenon of posthypnotic suggestion which we believe is very similar to a condition that takes place in the mind of the addict.

The hypnotist's subject is, to all intents and purposes, asleep. His conscious mind is not working, nor does the suggestion which is given to him under hypnosis appear in his conscious mind after waking. Let us see what happens in an experiment. The subject is hypnotized and told that he will take off his shoe promptly at eleven o'clock, which is two hours hence. He is awakened from his hypnotism, has no recollection of anything that took place, and promptly at eleven o'clock he starts to take off his shoe. When he is questioned about his reasons for removing his shoe, he replies, "I'm taking it off because my foot hurts." Here we have this man rationalizing an act which has been post-hypnotically suggested, because his conscious mind naturally seeks for a plausible explanation of why he is doing something without being aware of the reasons for his doing it. His answer has satisfied his conscious mind.

Let us compare the subject of this experiment with an addict whose mind has been anesthetized by alcohol. The desire to drink has been autosuggested just before he has become deeply intoxicated, and this suggestion acts in a manner similar to the suggestion made to the subject in hypnotic trance. Question the addicted drinker as to why he relapsed after a period of abstinence, and you will find that he will automatically rationalize his reasons for relapsing. He may tell you that he started to drink again because he lost his job, because his wife's nagging was insufferable, or because he had been treated unjustly or suspected of drinking when he had not. The rationalization always includes something in the environment as the reason for his beginning to drink again, and without insight into his own problem it is difficult for him to see that the impulses for the narcotic effect of alcohol were, like the posthypnotic suggestion, generated in his unconscious mind.

One woman who consulted me said, "I have been going to Dr. X, who hypnotized me. I found that while under the influence of his hypnotic suggestion I couldn't even enter a tavern without wishing to vomit. The idea of drinking was repulsive to me." I said to her, "If hypnotism is working so well as a treatment measure, why are you consulting me?" She replied, "There are times when I do not keep my appointments with Dr. X. Then I find I can go to a tavern and drink all I want, and very soon I am in as bad shape as ever. I am afraid I have to solve this problem myself, but I need your help to solve it."

Just as I attempted to manufacture a crutch against drinking by reminding myself of the terror of the experience of delirium tremens, so this woman reached out for the psychological crutch of hypnotism. In both our cases, the crutches worked for a time. This leads me to believe that crutches against drinking are not permanent curative tools.

Where a patient is cooperating with us, we have observed the phenomenon of dreams of an alcoholic nature, and interestingly enough, in no case have we found that these dreams occur until the period of abstinence. Over many years, I have questioned normal, controlled users of alcohol as to whether or not they have ever dreamed about alcohol, and their replies have always been negative. To them, alcohol is not emotionally important enough to dream about.

Let me cite a dream from which we may gain some insight into the formation of alcoholic impulses.

"I dreamt I was mortally wounded, and the doctor was just leaving after dressing my wound. He turned to my grief-stricken wife and said, 'He cannot live more than twenty-four hours.' After the doctor left, I turned to my wife and said, 'Go down and get the Scotch and soda. It cannot possibly make any difference now whether I drink or not, and we at least can make this death bed scene less distressing'."

I realize that some of my psychoanalytic friends might interpret this dream as an unconscious will for self-destruction due to a suppressed sexual complex that was incompatible with the ego ideal. In this instance, we uncovered nothing else to signify that this was the case, and I am inclined to accept the theory that in addiction an unconscious, peculiarly alcoholic conflict exists, a secondary dependency in the conscious mind. For instance, the mortal wound which was not self-inflicted points to an addicted drinker's characteristic escape mechanism; that is, he places the blame for his expected death on somebody else. This is purposive since many addicts have a conscious dread of dying from the immediate results of addicted drinking. The fear of death, due to abnormal drinking expresses the shame and guilt and fear of retribution that is felt by many addicts, but is not felt by the drinker where alcohol is not a critical problem, nor is it felt by the very unformed personality of the sociopath with an addiction problem.

First, then, in this alcoholic dream, the brunt of the responsibility is passed to someone else. Next we have the sentence, "He turned to my grief-stricken wife and said, 'He cannot live more than twenty-four hours'." The "grief-stricken wife" satisfies his need for love and affection. He is glad to see that she is grief-stricken, and due to the rather uncertain life he has given her, he has been unsure that she would be grief-stricken if he died. Not being able to live for more than twenty-four hours is another characteristic of the addicted drinker. He is avoiding the immediate issue and putting off until tomorrow the things that could have been done today, incidentally giving himself twenty-four hours in which to drink. The last part of the dream is a neat bit of unconscious rationalization. He says, "It cannot possibly make any difference now whether I drink or not," which from a physiological standpoint is true; but the neatest bit of all is the typical rationalization of making the deathbed scene less distressing by using alcohol.

Such a dream appears as the outcropping of an unconscious conflict over whether or not to drink again. The suggestion on the unconscious, absorbed during treatment, prohibited the less-complicated, wish-fulfillment alcoholic thought to emerge into consciousness, and the dream was resorted to as an escape from this suppressed desire. Because the escape found a loophole in a death scene, the dream need not only refer to a death wish, but also indicates the unconscious difficulty the drinker was experiencing in his search for loopholes which would permit him again to indulge in alcohol. It is interesting in this dream that the ego ideal is willing to accept oblivion to justify reindulgence.

In this patient, his intense application to treatment would not permit a simple wish-fulfillment dream. This dream gives us a clue to the fact that the patient has acquired through treatment more adequate defenses against alcoholic access to his regressive needs. He is not actually drinking, but the dream usually indicates deep unconscious resistance to recovery. These alcoholic dreams seem to fall into a rather general pattern. The patient dreams he has been drinking, with no clear picture of where or how. On awakening, he is anxious for a moment, has the feeling that the dream was real and that he actually had relapsed. We know that alcohol is a sick solution for filling the vacuum created by an incomplete ego and so have every reason to expect that the removal of the compromise will bring about a transitory state of conflict in its wake.

Unlike the neurotic's conflict that is exhibited by distressing symptoms, the addict's conflict is temporarily centered on whether or not to drink. If he can abstain from drinking with understanding help, then many of the emotional conflicts he was avoiding with the use of alcohol can be faced and understood with therapeutic help, whereas the neurotic's symptoms come from deeply suppressed conflicts, which take the form of incapacitating symptoms. We have in most cases of addicted drinking, the incomplete ego, where the conflicts necessary to personality development were avoided by various overcompensations in formative years, and as these overcompensations broke down in adult years, alcohol was progressively sought to buttress a crumbling personality structure.

I have a collection of alcoholic dreams which have been brought to me, in many of which I have become intoxicated in the most bizarre and degrading fashion. It is interesting to note that in these dreams the dreamer usually remains sober, devoting his full time and thoughtful care to the drunken image of his therapist. Such dreams offer us insight into the unconscious resistance that exists in the minds of our most cooperative patients. As a means of explanation, these dreams have a definite psychological value. The patient gains from a discussion of them an understanding of the insidious psychopathology that makes his addiction possible despite the terrific penalty that he knows he must pay for it.

Daydreams also give us a clue into the persistence of alcoholic impulses. For instance, I remember in the first part of World War II being consulted by a man who wished to go into the Navy and make a career of it. He knew that this career would be impossible unless he solved his addiction problem. Well along in treatment, he brought me the following daydream that he had had. He was in command of a destroyer. This ship had been torpedoed, and as he got into the life boat, he found that the water keg was stove in, and the only thing to drink was a case of Scotch whisky.

Another man at this period, going into the Army, and wishing to solve his drinking problem before he went in, brought me a daydream in which he was out in the desert. He had drunk his canteen of water and was dying of thirst. About that time, an army truck loomed into view, and he hailed it. The only thing they had to drink on board was a case of beer. My perhaps too flippant reply was, "You'd better be the man who carries two canteens of water instead of one."

As the purpose of this treatment plan unfolds itself to the cooperative patient, he brings up the various alcoholic thoughts, both direct and disguised, that have come to his mind, and from these thoughts we gain empirical data which suggest the proper treatment approach as discussed in a later chapter. We may reasonably expect that these thoughts will have sprung from (1) a wish to be able to drink normally; (2) a vague hope that some day he will be able to drink again, and (3) a hope that some sort of compromise can be worked out to permit partial indulgence.

These three dominating ideas may be expected to persist in spite of repeated proof by the addicted drinker to himself that he is not able to drink normally and who, in addition, has in all probability tried all the compromises of partial indulgence without having any of them work.

I remember many years ago talking to a group of young psychologists and psychiatrists in New York. I said to them, "If any of you want to be a charlatan and make a great deal of money, all you have to do is put on your shingle, 'I can teach the addicted drinker how to drink in moderation.' You will soon find that you have hundreds of patients with a drinking problem clamoring to get into your office." In due course, one of these men did just about that, and I am sure he had all the patients he could possibly handle, but I am equally sure that he never did any of them any good.

The resistance to recovery will persist for a long time. If the patient is responding to treatment, gaining the necessary understanding of his personality, he will still have decreasing impulses which he is able to bring to light for months and even years after the beginning of treatment. Let me quote from a cooperative patient who had been off alcohol for a long time.

I know it is ridiculous for me to have any reservations about drinking in the future. If anyone ever proved that alcohol created too rich a mixture for his psychic carburetor, I did, and yet thoughts spring to mind out of the thin air. They are not like direct alcoholic suggestions such as those which a cocktail party or a seductive advertisement creates. I know how to handle those. For no apparent reason, I start thinking of the possibility of my wife and children being killed in an automobile accident, and wondering if such a horrible incident would not be used by me as a legitimate reason to start drinking again. Or, I will think, "Suppose I am very successful now that I have given up alcohol, and am gaining self-respect and the esteem of my contemporaries, then I might start drinking in a normal, controlled manner." Sometimes the thought comes to mind that for the next five, ten, or twenty years, perhaps, I won't drink, and when I am an old man, I can start drinking again and it won't be a problem. Thoughts about a trip to Europe at some future date occur, and how impossible it seems to contemplate such a trip without drinking. I know I'm not going to Europe until I get the idea of no more alcohol as long as I live incorporated in my mental processes. However, the thought keeps occurring. Another thought has been that I would go off with a guide in the Canadian woods. No one would ever possibly know that I took a drink, and yet I know that if I did, I would ruin any possibility of hunting or fishing, both of which sports I am keenly interested in, and I also know that I would not terminate this drinking when I came out of the woods.

These resistant thoughts that all patients have should in

no way discourage us. In fact, we should be encouraged because the patient is sharing them with us.

I am convinced that a well-organized treatment plan is a fundamental requisite to the successful treatment of certain types of patients who are addicted to alcohol. It is true that in many of the complications of addicted drinking, and particularly in the organic ones, hospitals, sanitariums and other institutions serve a very valuable purpose: not to go beyond these is to court failure. Of necessity, institutions are custodial and protective, and this is inadequate preparation for the real struggle that is sure to come when the patient returns to his environment. Here the real battleground of life is encountered. His life with his sorrows and joys, perhaps complicated by a nagging or flirtatious wife, domineering parents, or difficult business partners, personal failures or successes; these are the offensive and defensive engagements that the partially readjusted personality must face. Too often, despite the insight and readjustment that a patient may have acquired in a sanitarium, his new approach and understanding will prove of little avail in facing the realities of his own environment. It is my thought, based on experience, that a patient discharged from a hospital should have someone whom he trusts and respects, with whom he can discuss these reality problems for a long time after he has left the hospital.

Based on my experience, I wish to emphasize the importance of continuing contact after the patient has been discharged from the hospital. I consider it vital to eventual recovery. As many of our patients come from a great distance, and as frequent commuting for follow-up treatment is difficult, we suggest to these patients that they stay in the open hospital for a longer time than we might recommend to local patients. When the patient has been discharged from the hospital and comes from a great distance, we recommend a psychiatrist in his vicinity who is familiar with our approach and will carry the patient in the very important outpatient therapeutic role. Such recommendation emphasizes that the acute psychological withdrawal symptoms that we may help the patient meet and understand are followed by secondary psychological withdrawal symptoms which, if not shared with professional understanding, can result in soul-shattering relapses.

In an attempt to sum up the many and varied individuals' response to having a critical problem with addicted drinking, I can do this best by illustrating with an incident.

The other day, I was asked by one of a group of medical students, to whom I was lecturing, to define "the alcoholic." My definition was, "Someone whose manner of drinking is interfering with his potential to pursue happiness in a healthy way." I am sure that this reply was not what the student had hoped for. Being a good student in the practice of internal medicine, he would have preferred a more specific answer, such as "a man or woman who drinks a fifth a day and shows certain neurological symptoms as a result of this intake of alcohol." Of course, damage to the body by excessive use of alcohol can and does occur, and should be treated by good medical skill. This aspect of the problem could have been found by the student in many medical text books. My reply to him was an attempt to lead him back to the previous hour's discussion, which had covered the facts that addiction to alcohol is a symptom as well as a cause of personality maladjustment, and that any readjustment is impossible as long as the patient clings to this symptom; i.e., the patient's drinking is a faulty, sick way to pursue happiness, but because of his personality maladjustment it seems to him the only way. Fortunately, as I believe, the potentiality to pursue happiness in a healthy way is latently there in many patients, and can be brought out with the proper help.

Chapter IV

FURTHER IDENTIFICATION
OF THE ADDICTED DRINKER

The markings of the addicted drinker are not so plain as might be expected, and the conception of the man in the street is usually far from accurate. The term *alcoholic* has become as vague and meaningless as the words *nervous breakdown,* or the feminine *vapors* of the nineteenth century. To the public, an alcoholic presents a picture of a bleary-eyed, bulbous-nosed, shaky creature, disheveled and uncombed, often in the hands of a burly policeman who is ushering him none too gently into the depths of a patrol wagon. Should the curious attend magistrates' courts, they will see the same shaky individual sentenced to the House of Correction, which sentence is sometimes accompanied by a "wise crack" from "His Honor," who finds and appeals to the low sense of his court's humor by some scathing remarks about the unfortunate drunkard's condition.

This poor chap, while he is certainly drunken, may merely have the symptoms of some form of mental illness. In a large city, he may belong to the so-called nomadic type, representing a group made up of men who have developed no true home ties, have severed family bonds and relinquished social attachments. Usually they are borderline mental cases, and

49

the alcoholic display is a comparatively unimportant episode of much more important mental abnormality.

In any event, the individual's concept of abnormal drinking is very apt to be colored by personal experience. It may be based on having been pressed into service to rescue a business or club friend on a spree, from some dive or from a hotel room where he periodically engages in long bouts of solitary drinking. There may be an addiction problem in the family, and if so, the conclusion concerning the nature of addicted drinking is derived from a long and painful association with the drinking relative. Naturally, opinions arrived at on the basis of a single or a few instances are very likely to be erroneous.

In any classification scheme employed in a clinic devoted to the treatment of addicted drinking, there are many diagnostic terms. This means simply that overindulgence in alcohol may occur at some time or another in many separate conditions. One must be careful not to label indiscriminately all these conditions as addicted drinking. For instance, drinking to excess often occurs in actual mental disease. In one phase of insanity called mania, the patient is extremely exuberant, overly social and on the very "crest of the wave." Thoughts seem to rush through his mind with the speed of a streamlined locomotive, and this patient is very likely to celebrate with an alcoholic debauch. The debauch in itself has very little significance in the mental illness, and it would be as stupid to treat it alone and expect the patient to get well as it would be to give a patient who had a headache due to a brain tumor a few doses of aspirin, or to put an ice cap on his head and expect him to recover from the brain tumor. The same thought would apply to melancholia, the contrasting phase of this form of mental disease. Here, the patient is deeply depressed, and, if he has enough initiative, he may try to drown his mental suffering in liquor. We can state with accuracy, in order to begin to limit the concept of addicted drinking to its proper boundaries, that whenever actual mental disease exists, the addicted drinking is not pathological drinking *per se,* but merely a relatively unimportant phenomenon of the underlying mental abnormality. The single exception is mental illness due to alcoholic excesses.

The same situation applies to the drinking that may occur in mental defect or feeblemindedness. The moron has a simple brain pattern, usually congenital, and he is incapable of rising above a childish level of intelligence. Through imitation, or because he may not have sufficient protection in life, he may drink to excess. This will not be because he is an addicted drinker, but because he is feebleminded.

I would like to call particular attention to a group in which alcoholic overindulgence is fairly common. The members of this group are certainly unfitted for the method of treatment which we advocate, and, indeed, scarcely respond to any form of therapy. I refer to what psychiatry calls the sociopathic personality. Although diagnostic terms are necessary in a specialty like psychiatry, I feel very strongly that there is danger in such labels because they tend to group people with behavioral disorders, and hence, the inclination is to treat this group as if they all sprang from the same personality mold. Degree is all-important. After all, there are in all of us latent sociopathic trends, hangovers from our primitive infantile phase, but we developed enough ego strength to keep up a pretty good defense against our primitive selves. However, it does not take psychiatric diagnosis to reveal that under the influence of too much alcohol these defenses start crumbling.

In order to avoid using this diagnostic term, *sociopath,* I shall refer to this group as personalities arrested on a primitive level at which their ego has not formed to a point where they have feelings of guilt, shame, or remorse, or any feelings of responsibility toward their fellowman. In a few words, they are individuals who, though they are often engaging and charming in manner and not at all intellectually defective, are, nevertheless, grossly defective in practically all the other functions of the mind and personality, unstable in their emotions, defective in their judgment, deficient in their ethics and, in short, totally inadequate and unreliable in their response to social reactions and behavior.

In this group are included many of the individuals who consult us from some ulterior motive, perhaps to avoid a divorce or to escape punishment by simulating a desire to rehabilitate themselves. Dr. Lawrence Kolb* says, "A common type among these cases (psychopathic characters) is a psychopath who, with his special deviation of personality, is, in the language of the street, an individual who knows it all and does not care." When we have attempted treatment with this type, we inevitably uncover the following characteristics which make the continuance of treatment impossible. First, they undertake the treatment with an assurance of success which we find lacking in most of the sincere patients who successfully terminate their abnormal drinking. Second, they are either unable or unwilling to conform to one of the fundamental prerequisites of this form of psychotherapy which is strict truthfulness with the therapist. Third, this type of personality is unable to cooperate. They make the gesture toward helping themselves—but a careful check on our part shows that it is all gesture.

All in all, the personalities arrested on a primitive growth level are completely lacking in truthfulness and sincerity. They are not sincere about a will to get well; consequently, the reeducational methods that we advocate are never followed. Their inner philosophy seems to be: "Why do I need reeducation when I really know all the answers? However, I will play along with the treatment in order to satisfy my rich

*"Types and Characteristics of Drug Addicts," by LAWRENCE KOLB, M.D. From *Mental Hygiene,* Vol. IX, No. 2, April. 1925, pp. 300-313. The National Committee for Mental Hygiene, Inc., New York City.

wife or irate father."

The following is a typical example of a primitive arrestment complicated by addictive drinking. The patient was sent to us by a physician in one of the southern cities. Mr. M. was badly in need of medical care and supervision when he arrived in Philadelphia and submitted to hospitalization. The reports from the hospital were that he was cooperative. At the first interview with me he said that he did not realize until the last debauch that alcohol had such a hold on him. He now knew, due to his immediate past experience, that he was a drunkard, and he wished to take up treatment so that he could give up alcohol forever. When he was questioned regarding his past drinking and life history, certain omissions of truth became more and more evident, and later on in treatment these lapses in truthfulness became increasingly conspicuous. On checking over the history of this man, we found that he had spent several months during each year of the past five years taking various "cures," sobering up in order to permit a reindulgence in alcohol. All of this he failed to mention in giving his history. After a comparatively short time, he relapsed, and though it was perfectly obvious that he had been indulging in alcohol, he tried to deceive us by pretending an illness which had nothing to do with alcohol. Eventually, the truth came out. He had committed a criminal offense during a period of intoxication. The man whom he had injured was convinced by him that alcohol was the sole cause of the criminal act and had told him that if he would pull himself together and overcome his abnormal drinking, he would not be prosecuted. Obviously, there was no real incentive on the patient's part to get well, and our consulting rooms were merely being used as a lesser of two evils, jail or treatment.

If those with an ego arrestment on a primitive level have one consistent trait, it is an unwillingness to tell the truth. They are psychiatry's prize liars. Because most drinkers will lie defensively about their drinking to their husbands, wives, or business associates, they are not to be confused for this reason with those whose ego arrestment is on a primitive level. Let us say that the recoverable addict lies about his addiction but is, generally speaking, quite truthful about other things that pertain to his life.

One encounters a widespread pessimistic or defeatist view about helping addicted drinkers, a great deal of which is due to these psychopathic characters. They are not fit subjects for psychological reeducation and often exert a destructive influence on sincere men who are earnestly endeavoring to overcome alcoholic addiction. This type must be separated in diagnosis from the addicted drinker who can be helped. The sociopath is a crippled personality in which a capacity for even a fractional response to treatment has been destroyed or never existed, and it is as futile to expect from him a sincere application to a reeducational program as it would be to expect a one-legged man to run a race. It is hoped that effective treatment may one day be found for these primitive emotional arrestments because, with or without a drinking problem, they are a considerable threat to society.

It has been clearly indicated that not every individual who gets drunk is to be considered an addicted drinker either in the sense of proper diagnosis or from the standpoint of hopeful treatment. In addition to the mentally sick, the mentally defective, and those arrested on a primitive growth level, there are other groups, certain types of personality, which do not respond satisfactorily to our reeducative treatment. This may be because the drinking is not the basic issue and is merely the surface expression of an underlying illness quite remote from addicted drinking. Sometimes patients are not capable of meeting attempts at treatment with even the rudiments of cooperation.

In this group, for instance, would fall certain individuals who, while they may not be mentally sick, nevertheless present grave personality defects. There is an aggressive type, temperamentally antisocial and inconsiderate. Alcohol unleashes seriously aggressive behavior, and "in his cups" he presents the traditional picture of the "fighting drunk" who may become homicidal. There is an adynamic, dull type, made up of those who have little or no ambition or drive and are usually at a low economic level, and a primitive type, made up of individuals also living at a very low economic level, whose behavior is largely instinctive and whose reactions appear in extremely simple patterns. Neither of these groups is amenable to treatment since they are scarcely able to grasp the intellectual approach that we recommend and, furthermore, the accustomed hand-to-mouth existence destroys the incentive for recovery. It is not to be inferred that a high degree of intelligence is needed before a patient dare embark on our plan of treatment. Ordinary intelligence and a moderate degree of common sense is quite sufficient.

There remains a very large segment quite favorable for treatment. The important component, both quantitatively and qualitatively, of this segment is the potentiality to strengthen the ego. As the theme is developed, we will furnish more accurate distinguishing marks in the effort to discover those who may be greatly helped by a plan of psychological reeducation.

An exhibition of drunkenness by an individual often means as little in terms of psychological appreciation as does headache or fever, in the understanding of the underlying bodily illness. It is much more important to discern the drives and trends that are uncovered by the addicted drinking. Much can be learned from the patient himself by asking him to describe his mental reactions in the early phases of his drinking. Equally important are consultations with wife, husband, or close friends of the patient, in order to obtain a clear picture of the abnormalities exhibited during the drinking episode. From the beginning it is important to find potentialities for readjustment. It would be splendid if every

man or woman who drinks to excess could be cured, but for
many reasons, and mainly because many of them are not
basically addicted drinkers, we cannot expect such sweeping
results from psychological reeducation.

The term *normal drinker* is not paradoxical. In a previous
chapter devoted to the intoxication impulse, it was explained
that the drinker gains a childlike state of mind. He finds his
moods susceptible to his environment. He is, in truth, more
childlike because he has anesthetized the inhibiting faculties
gained in the process of acquiring a mature response to
reality. If he is normal, he presents a picture of a convivial
drinker who uses alcohol as a socially acceptable gesture and
never gets into serious trouble from its use. His drinking is
done solely to bring about a state of mind in which his
thought processes are less strictly inhibited. He gains freedom
from the conformity to the behavior demanded by maturity
and is, therefore, more childlike and naive. He cajoles his
subjective self in some such fashion as this: "Let's make
believe that life is all happiness, and I, with a few cocktails
under my belt, am one of the most contented, charming and
intelligent members of my group. The fact that I have a wart
on my misshapen nose is more than compensated for by my
intelligence and charm." This utopia vanishes with sobriety,
and though the sober personality is painfully aware of the
wart on the nose and keenly realizes that he is woefully
lacking in the charm and intelligence he craves, he nevertheless accepts the reality of sobriety because he is, in fact, well-
adjusted to it.

The borderline between normal and abnormal drinking is
crossed when a man attempts to use alcohol as an aid to
adjust himself to reality. The first symptoms of this
dangerous and abnormal use of alcohol may be transitory or
may be the beginning of an eventual addiction problem.

Early danger signals appear in various guises. For instance,
we notice that the conversation of one of our friends, whom

we have always considered a normal, well-behaved and reserved person, becomes embarrassingly indecent after a few drinks. Another friend, ordinarily modest and retiring, becomes extremely boastful under the same condition. Still others who used to be friendly and cheerful become more and more retiring. Occasionally we see someone who is usually friendly and gregarious suddenly become rude and gauche after he has had a few highballs.

In the peculiarities of these reactions, we believe that there is revealed a glimpse of the attempt of the ego to compensate for certain conflicts not acceptable to the ego ideal of the individual. It is as if the intoxicated person unconsciously knew that by narcotizing the higher nervous centers, too much of the inner man would be revealed to the judgment of his fellows, and so he attempts to compensate for maladjustments of personality, normally unadmitted, even to himself.

Sometimes the conversation of a drinker who becomes embarrassingly indecent may lead you to suspect that he is suffering from a sex complex, for it is true that the unfortunate who attempts to convey the impression of potency is usually insecure in his own feelings of sexual adequacy. The boaster who brags of his prowess in the business world when he has "drink taken" is insecure in his innermost feelings about his ability, and is endeavoring to reassure both you and himself. The man who becomes rude and gauche is merely trying to hide his social insecurity by attacking first, because he constantly fears that a social offensive may be launched against him. Thus, one of the hazards of alcohol is that without conscious deliberation it may be readily applied as a salve which in the beginning, at least, acts magically in soothing the painful wounds of personal belittlement and insignificance.

In this connection, we must not accept the old adage, *in vino veritas* too literally, as it would require a trained psychotherapist to analyze the drunken babble of many alcoholized persons. If this babble reveals anything, it is that alcohol is the great uninhibitor and releases material from depths which otherwise would never have reached the surface. What we must accept in the individual whose drinking has become a problem to his friends, his family and himself is that he is undoubtedly tending to use alcohol for its psychological compensatory power as an escape from, rather than as an exaggeration of reality. Whether such a person is definitely recognized as an addicted drinker, or as a bad actor or an ineffective worker, because of the use of alcohol, makes little difference in the ultimate seriousness of his problem. In any event, abnormal drinking, if it continues, reveals a state of mind which the drinker himself regards as unendurable.

Those who know little of the psychology of abnormal drinking are easily deceived by the camouflage which the addicted drinker unconsciously uses to disguise his maladjustment. It is true that many addicted drinkers have, in their actual circumstances, a good excuse for employing the escape mechanism offered by alcohol. However, it is rare to find the real underlying cause of an addiction entirely contained in the immediate environment. When we question our patients, they either do not know why they use alcohol abnormally, or they attempt to rationalize the use of it. We who are approaching the addicted drinker in the first interview know only one thing—the patient has developed a problem of addiction to alcohol. It has been my experience that the approach I am indicating in this book is effective for a group of patients whose addicted drinking is a symptom of an unfinished growth step in their struggle to form an adequate, workable personality.

Both the neurotic symptoms and the abnormal drinking symptoms stem from difficulties in forming a reality-facing personality. The psychiatrist's role is to help the neurotic patient gain insight which will eventually enable the patient to discard his neurotic symptoms by helping him to see that the symptom was functionally purposive; that is, the patient unknowingly developed a crippling symptom in order to escape facing intolerable conflict.

Though alcohol may at times be used to ward off neurotic symptoms, it is my belief that we find in the addicted drinker a more primitive symptom which I would call preneurotic. What do I mean by preneurotic as compared to neurotic? The neurotic patient in his developing years was able to have conflict as part of a necessary growth struggle, but was unable to handle it satisfactorily, whereas the developing years of the addicted drinker reveal a technique of avoiding conflict. The addicted drinking patient usually is found to have developed in his formative years a technique of manipulating the environment so that he or she did not have to conform, and often the parents, because of their own personality difficulties, acquiesced in the nonconformity of their child. Hence, the child missed a great deal of necessary conflict in developing years.

The crisis seems to come for both the psychoneurotic and the addicted drinker in their adult years. The addicted drinker has found that the adults in his life are rejecting his old tried-and-true manipulation techniques. They won't buy them any more. He has met his Waterloo, so what does he do? He says, "I can no longer manipulate the environment so I'll have a go at manipulating myself," and he discovers that the abnormal use of alcohol will permit him to do this. "If I can't get realities to accept me in the way that I wish them to accept me, I can by indulgence in alcohol create the illusion that the old manipulation technique is still working." It is the psychiatrist's and my job to help the patient see this, understand it, and because he has gained insight, struggle to relinquish these destructive emotional techniques that were crippling his potentiality to adjust in a healthy way.

The pictures that present themselves to us vary from those who are not even suspected by their contemporaries of being abnormal drinkers to others whose trouble, no one can doubt, has to do with alcohol and plenty of it. In a group of unevident addicted drinkers, we usually find that the condition has been disguised from the world by the connivance of the family who dread the stigma that would be attached to the spreading of the knowledge that a son, brother, husband, or wife is psychologically dependent on alcohol. Such a precarious status of protection may persist for a long time, the periods of abnormal drinking being explained away under the heading of some "nervous" or other illness. In such cases, unwise families are aiding and abetting a condition which they are too proud to face frankly and honestly, and as the progress of the disorder invariably brings it to the light of society in a conspicuous fashion, they have accomplished nothing of a beneficial nature and usually they have done a great deal of harm. From the top of the ladder of social approval down to the last rung of social condemnation, we may expect to find the condition of addicted drinking.

Symptoms are evident in those who refuse to face any phase of reality without recourse to alcohol. These are the men and women who must start drinking for "courage" to face the day, and must continue to drink in order to "carry on" through the day. Just because they can refrain from using alcohol for varying lengths of time after the distress of an alcoholic breakdown that demanded medical care and supervision is no reason for them or their friends to think that they can again drink in moderation. Popular belief to the contrary, severe cases of addicted drinking often go "on the wagon" for surprisingly long periods of time. This is not so remarkable when one takes into consideration the tremendous immediate incentive produced by the distress of the relapse. This is a suppression of addicted drinking, and the addiction-conditioned reaction is still in being, but temporarily smothered under by high resolve and promises to live a sober life. Unfortunately, hopeful families become optimistic during these periods of abstinence, believing that a "cure" has been effected, only to have their optimism shattered by the inevitable relapse and the re-creation of an increasingly vicious circle of drunkenness, medical supervision, periods of abstinence and then drunkenness again.

A less obvious, but equally serious type of addicted drinker, is the one whose behavior becomes unsocial as soon as he starts to drink. Though his friends may excuse his conduct as only being caused by intoxication, he is, generally speaking, an increasingly annoying nuisance and bore, as well as an embarrassment at social gatherings. In young men such symptoms, when they are quite frequent and critical, usually herald the condition of definitely addicted drinking.

Again, there is the semi-invalid type, usually a narcissistic individual whose personality refuses to permit the out-and-out earmarks of drunkenness. Consequently, he lives a Dr. Jekyll and Mr. Hyde existence, presenting to his environment the picture of a semi-invalid drinking in a controlled manner, only to unleash deeper addiction in the privacy of his home. Eventually, he, too, is "caught out" because of the progressive abnormality of his drinking.

Sooner or later the excessive drinker with the least shred of intelligence is forced to face the fact that his drinking is abnormal, and this is the crucial psychological moment when he really has a chance of absorbing and applying the reeducation that is necessary to permit him to lead an adequate nonalcoholic existence. The self-diagnosed addicted drinker is always the one about whom we are most optimistic.

The recoverable addicted drinker is the man with a sick dependency on alcohol who is attempting to face reality and who asks for professional help to enable him to discard this addiction and to face the reality from which he has been running away.

There is no absolute rule by virtue of which alcohol may

be used safely and sanely. However, a self-inventory along the following lines can help you to analyze whether or not you are an addicted drinker:

1. In your frank judgment, and in the honest opinion of your friends, have there been personality changes since your early drinking days? If so, this is dangerous.

2. Consider the history of your drinking. Is it about the same level of moderate, controlled drinking as it was in the beginning, or has it increased considerably? If it has increased considerably, this is dangerous.

3. What do you gain by drinking? Is that gain something upon which you are too dependent? If so, this is dangerous.

4. Do you realize that your drinking is becoming progressively too important to you? If so, this is dangerous.

Chapter V

PSYCHOLOGICAL MECHANISMS
IN ADDICTED DRINKING

Freud and his colleagues in their pioneer endeavors to understand the motivations of the mentally ill, as well as the emotional motivations of the so-called normal man, reached the conclusion that much of man's behavior stemmed from what they termed the *Unconscious;* that is, that man was influenced in his response to himself and his environment by emotional sources beneath his conscious level of awareness. The picture he gave his students of the unconscious showed with brutal frankness that it was free of moral standards and contained a lack of ethical standards which was equivalent to the behavior of the higher apes. This concept was more than the intelligentsia of the fading Victorian era could take. They had already been disturbed by Darwin's theory of evolution, and were unable to accept that they, the proper Victorians, still retained in their unconscious the primitive instincts of their apelike ancestors. Therefore, Freud's concept was met with hostility, rage, condemnation and ridicule, and this persists to some degree to this day. Fortunately for society, there were enough physicians specializing in the treatment of mental illness to explore Freud's work, and to find that his ideas were useful to them in understanding their patients' illnesses.

It has been said that man is but the child grown, which I have endeavored to bring out in some detail in the following diagram. This pictures with necessary oversimplification the concept of the emotional complex that we are faced with in the process of growing up, developing a personality, and living out our lives as fairly well adjusted human beings. I have done this by drawing a pyramid, starting with the bottom step as a foundation of the personality in infancy and progressing in steps to the older adult.

You will note that in the diagram I have indicated that the primitive feelings of the infant in Step #1, and to a lesser degree in Step #2 are later repressed to unconscious levels because the maturing personality in its growth steps is gradually pressing the primitive feelings of the infant down below the surface of awareness where they are incorporated in the no-man's-land as part of the unconscious. However, the fact that they have been repressed does not mean that they are not still there. We get a glimpse of them in our analyzed dreams and our wishes, and sometimes our actions under intense emotional pressure, as well as in grave mental illness where we see the individual acting out and living in much of the primitive infantile unconscious.

In less grave mental illness, we find regression also, but to a lesser degree, and in abnormal drinking we have the interesting phenomenon of the personality regressing via the introduction of the intoxicants. In these cases, sobriety brings a return of reality, but a reality that is so painful to the maladjusted individual that reindulgence in alcohol, in order to regress, becomes more and more necessary. The point I wish to make is that addicted drinking is just as much a mental illness, and hence in need of understanding help, as the grave mental illness called psychosis, and the less grave mental illness called psychoneurosis.

In order to simplify the comparison between the grave mental illness, the psychosis, on the one hand, and the less grave mental illness, the psychoneurosis, and addicted drinking on the other, we can say that the psychotic is out of

Approximate Age
23–up
6 Older Adult:

Continuous ability to adapt to the adult role. Include the responsibility of supporting oneself and family, and the ability to cope with inevitable failures and frustrations as well as success.

Approximate Age
17–22 years
5 Young Adult:

The young adult has developed a personality which is conditioned by the previous growth steps.

Approximate Age
11–17 years
4 Adolescence:

The child is in a period of stormy transition. Sex urges become much more pressing. There is a good deal of conflict about these urges. It is a period when the growing personality is making a choice of being adult or clinging to previous childlike levels.

Approximate Age
6–11 years
3 Second Stage
of Childhood:

More conflict is expressed. The child will at times test the omnipotence of the parents by defying openly or by more subtle techniques, such as lying or by attempting to deceive the adult parents.

Approximate Age
2–6 years
2 Early Childhood:

Still a good deal of primitive acting out. The child has started to identify itself with the parents, and is expressing conflict between the primitive self and the struggle to identify with the adults. Much of this period is relegated to the unconscious.

Approximate Age
0–2 years
1 Infant:

Infancy is obviously the first step in the formation of a personality. The infant is dependent on the adult's care, and we find that the infant has a very animal-like, instinctive approach to its environment. Because this level of growth is so primitive, it is repressed gradually in childhood, and is more and more relegated to the unconscious.

touch with reality, and the psychoneurotic is largely in touch with reality except for his neurotic symptoms, which cause a segment of his personality to be out of touch with reality. The type of mental illness we are treating here is one of many symptoms indicating a personality maladjustment. The psychoneurotic may have unreasonable fears or the need to perform some compulsive act, just as the addicted drinker has the need to overindulge in alcohol. But here the likeness of the addicted drinker and the psychoneurotic draw apart. It is true that both the psychoneurotic symptoms and abnormal drinking are interfering with the adequate functioning of the personality, but the addicted drinker turns to an outside agent, alcohol. This he uses in an abnormal way which interferes with his potentiality for adequate adjustment. Hence, we cannot say that abnormal drinking is a symptom of a psychoneurosis. It is an entity, a form of maladjustment with its own symptoms, which are peculiar to itself.

Unlike neurotic symptoms stemming from conflict that the patient is unable to face because they are below his conscious level, it seems as if the abnormal drinker is avoiding conflicts that he never met and resolved as part of his growth struggle to form an adequate personality. The average person who does not suffer from these minor mental illnesses is intolerant of such symptoms, and is apt to advise, "Get hold of yourself," or "Why don't you use a little will power?" He does not realize that these symptoms are deeply imbedded in emotional maladjustments of which the patient is completely unaware and that it may take prolonged professional help before the patient can understand and discard these symptoms.

Although I am dealing in this book with only one aspect of mental illness, addicted drinking, it should not be difficult for the reader to identify this condition with other mental symptoms. Looking at the diagram of emotional growth steps that we go through to develop a personality adequate to cope maturely with reality, we can see how important each growth step is toward the adequate development of a complete personality. The importance of the parents on whom the infant and the child are dependent must be self-evident.

The complexities of helping the infant, the child and the adolescent to form an adequate personality over a period of many years involve a great deal of love and understanding from the parents. Let us think of the parents as a team of architects and of the infant as an unskilled laborer under their direction. At first, he has little to go on but instinct. The parental architects often design much too massive or elaborate mansions for this unskilled laborer, or perhaps they were uninterested in the finished product, or one or the other died before the job was started, or the parental team of architects broke up the firm by divorce; or perhaps one of the firm quit on the job by developing a drinking problem, or by becoming mentally ill. At best, we parents, the architects, are so full of faults that the amazing thing is that the child often adapts so well in spite of our faulty blueprints. Let your imagination play with the countless facets of the two architects and the green builder, and you should come up with the greatest respect for the adjustment that the child may make, and a better understanding of the maladjustment that is so easy to make.

Take the green builder of the personality. He begins life completely dependent, and has to be fed and changed and loved, and cuddled. He is going through the phase of his growth where he is completely dependent. As he grows, many new ingredients and challenges are added. One of these ingredients is discomfort. At first, it may be physical, but this is very soon followed by emotional discomfort. The infant is pretty helpless. He must yell for help when discomfort appears, and the mother parent rushes to supply first aid for his discomfort. Her first aid kit consists of warm milk for hunger pains or dexterity in removing the offending safety pin, plus love and common sense and instinct.

It is easy to see that some mothers do not have very good first aid kits. Perhaps through no fault of their own, they may not be able to supply warm milk from themselves, or they may not know how to remove the offending safety pin, or they may be so in love with themselves that they have little to spare for their babies, or they may be deficient in common sense. The father architect in his own emotional attitude to a child can be the cause of just as many emotional difficulties as the mother in the child's struggle to form an adequate personality. One fact is sure: a deficiency in either architect's personality will eventually show in the builder of the new personality. Adaptable as a human being is, and adroit at the art of compensation, and facile in plastering over faulty construction, the faulty structure will eventually begin to reveal itself at any time from childhood to old age.

We are interested here in one form of personality breakdown: addicted drinking. What is more understandable than that the builder of the faulty personality, unaware of the bad architecture and bad blueprints, pursues happiness in a very different way from a better-adjusted adult. The addicted drinker unconsciously goes back to the dependency level of the infant, and the effect produced by deep intoxication permits him to capture a dependency satisfaction. In order to understand the problem of addicted drinking, one must have an understanding of the emotional regression that can be induced by deep intoxication.

I repeat that man is but the child grown, and this may be taken to mean that the man carries with him unresolved growth steps denied him in his struggle to form an adequate personality. This creates deficiencies in personality formation. Not having experienced some of the emotional growth steps such an individual goes through, he develops an early form of maladjustment which permits him to function, but such maladjustment makes him increasingly uncomfortable as he reaches adult years. I heartily disagree with the attempts that are made to relate addicted drinking to any one causative pattern. I say only that in the background of the addicted drinker there is always difficulty in forming an adequate personality. The reasons for this will be myriad, and the outcome and extent of treatment will largely depend on the period when the difficulties of forming a personality were encountered, as well as on the extent of these difficulties.

Parental mistakes are inevitable and seem to do no great harm, provided that the parents are willing to share the growth struggle of the child with understanding and love. Unhappily, in this industrialized era, the sharing of the child's growth struggle is more difficult than it was fifty or a hundred years ago. Truly, the monster of the machine era is destroying much of our mental health in the most subtle manner. In this competitive world, at all cultural and economic levels of our society, it is hard to find the time to share the growth struggle of our children.

This brings me to an all-important concept, that one very common causative factor of addicted drinking symptoms in the adult is an expression of some deep unconscious feeling of rejection developed in the course of the child's growth struggle. When we think of rejection of the child by the parents, we are apt to think in oversimplified terms such as the baby left in a basket on the orphanage steps, or the mother who ran off with a traveling salesman, deserting her children, or the father who deserted his wife and family.

Traumatic feelings of rejection in the formative years are not often this obvious, though my case records do include all the aforementioned episodes. More frequently, feelings of rejection are engendered in less dramatic ways. However, they leave their influence on the unconscious and show this influence in later emotional discomfort that can often reflect itself in abnormal drinking. Many intelligent adults have difficulty in accepting this concept of rejection because they, being adults with a highly developed capacity to accept reality, find it hard to place themselves in the role of the child who has little if any capacity to accept such grim realities as divorce, death, or chronic illness of a parent. More subtle rejection feelings are engendered in childhood by the ambitious father in the business world or the professions who devotes so much of his time to his work that his children have little time to feel his companionship and love, while frequently his wife, socially ambitious, also has little time to share in her children's growing up.

In the early years of working with patients with a drinking problem, I would frequently hear from parents of these patients, many of them highly successful in their fields, "I have given this boy (or girl) everything. Why did this happen to my child?" I used to speculate that these parents did give the child all the material things of life, but I discovered later in treatment that the parents gave the child everything but what the child really needed and wanted, that is, companionship, love and understanding, and the necessary right to share his growth struggle with his parents.

I wish to stress that often feelings of rejection which were unavoidable are by no means deliberately caused by the parents. Certainly the death or chronic illness of a parent is no one's fault. The father and mother who both work in order to be able to give the child the best education their means can provide have good motives, but they frequently ignore the fact that the child needs their intimate contact far more than an expensive education in order to grow a sound personality.

Patients will frequently pose an interesting question, as follows: "Why did I make a mess of my life when my brothers and sisters seemed to make adequate adjustments? What makes me different from them?" As the patient gains insight, he will become aware that there are always reasons why he or she had greater difficulty in forming an adequate personality than their brothers or sisters. Sometimes the patient is the eldest child, sometimes a middle child, and sometimes the youngest child in a family group. I think it is perfectly understandable that difficulties in adjustment will be encountered in a child at a certain age while an older or younger sibling may adjust without too much difficulty. For instance, the death or divorce of a parent might be a very shattering experience to a child of a certain age and not nearly so important and upsetting in the adjustment of a younger or older child. Again, the birth of a brother or sister may have a far more disturbing effect on the previous youngest, whereas his older brothers and sisters with more formed personalities may adjust and adapt to this new personality in the family with relative ease. The youngest child of the family is all at once presented with a rival for the love and affection he has demanded and secured from his parents.

I could fill this book with case records to fortify the concept that experiences in formative years very often play a great part in addicted drinking in later adult life. When you study the effects of alcohol on the emotional feelings of the adult, you see that alcohol is the great rejection solvent. Feelings of insecurity are feelings we all have at times. What is important is what we do to overcome these painful feelings. For instance, if we miss a promotion that we think we deserved, we may have to work harder to obtain this promotion at a later date, or we may change jobs. The important thing in the response to feelings of rejection is to have the capacity to endure emotional discomfort, to live with it, and do what we can to solve it even if solving it takes months or years.

The personalities with a drinking problem cannot take this approach. Because, in their formative years, feelings of rejection were written off as part of their personality that they could do nothing about and therefore had to live with, they blindly look as adults for the panacea, the universal medicine that will relieve these feelings. Alcohol, a mighty handy medicine, is readily accessible in the store, the bottle, or the tavern. Addicted drinkers' lack of capacity to deal with frustrations, failures and rejection form a very important part of their personality maladjustments. A patient must understand this in order to see the source of the problem and to gain insight for dealing with it in a more adult way, if he is to expect to be able to relinquish alcohol as a sick personality crutch.

Much has been written and exhaustive studies have been made by my psychoanalytical colleagues of the emotional interplay of the child and the parents. I do not wish to imply that each parent should be psychoanalyzed before being able to do an adequate job. However, an awareness of our own unconscious feelings toward our children might help us avoid some of the mistakes caused by too great repression of our own responses to infants, children, and adolescents.

The superficial view of a patient who has been sober for weeks gives little or no clue to underlying drinking abnormalities. Many of our patients are potentially capable of meeting reality and, indeed, are often superior in endowment. Perhaps we have overlooked the possibility of a degree of abnormality that is contained neither in mental disease nor in the neurosis, but is obtained only by the use of toxic agents that alter the ways of thinking and being.

Could it be that many addicted drinkers are so because they are perhaps too stable to become insane or to accept the minor psychosis which we call the neurosis? Having made bad adjustments to environment, have they unconsciously discovered in alcohol an escape that would be denied them without the use of this toxic agent? I believe this is frequently the case. It seems reasonable to believe that a large segment of abnormal drinking is due to a badly formed personality. Many addicted drinkers are capable of facing life quite successfully, even though they feel insecure and distrust their capacities. Threatened defeat in the battle of life is anticipated and to some extent discounted by the expedient of setting their subjective standards too high. Thus, the insult to the ego is lessened. From a normal, objective point of view, they are not inferior personalities, but only think themselves inferior because with unconscious purpose they have placed their standards so much higher than the average.

The proof of this is to be found in many who, no matter how badly they themselves may have failed in taking their rightful place in reality, always expect and demand too much of those who have made adequate adjustments. It seems as if they are unwilling to compromise with life, and their philosophy is, "If I can't be perfect, why try to be anything? However, I do expect and demand perfection in those who have the audacity to pretend that they have made an adequate adjustment."

Where there is incomplete formation of a personality in formative years, and one develops into an addicted drinker, we may see how he, too, uses destructively the state of mind that demands perfection in others, and for a long time his attitude of, "Who are you to tell me what to do?" will be a stumbling block in the way of his submission to treatment. If the psychiatrist is a moderate drinker, the patient at once pounces on this fact, refusing to recognize that there are plenty of people who can drink in moderation in a controlled manner. He can see in the gesture of drinking in others only the morbid condition that exists in regard to his own drinking. Such a state of mind, super-critical concerning those who are trying to help him, is, of course, a resistance on the part of the abnormal drinker against getting well, as it is, too, a symptom of the immature level on which the personality has chosen to face life. This is perhaps akin to the gradual dawning in the mind of a child of the knowledge that his mother and father are not omnipotent, and the subsequent shock that takes place when he finds that his parents are of but the same clay of which other adults are fashioned. One wonders if this recruit for the army of addicted drinkers, unconsciously clinging to regressive levels, did not have a frightening glimpse in childhood of the full burden that would be demanded of him if he allowed himself to mature and if, being untrained and uninformed as to how to accept maturity, he did not then rebel and cling to an immature level. Subsequently, his lot is thrown with people who have adjusted to maturer levels, and his position becomes uncomfortable and untenable. To compensate for this, he develops a system of escapes which he hopes will be acceptable to his environment.

I am encouraged when a new patient tells me that he has had periods "on the wagon" or has attempted to limit his drinking. This shows that there is enough development of his personality so that he wishes to defend it from the regressive needs he indulges in when he drinks. Some of the defenses used prior to the treatment are somewhat as follows: periods "on the wagon"; determination never to drink before the sun crosses the yardarm; only to drink with the wife or husband before dinner; minimum drinking of beer or light wine, or only taking one drink a day, or only drinking on weekends, or determining not to drink except on vacations.

The fact that these inadequate defenses have been tried and proved futile is frequently the reason that the patient seeks professional help. The defense of regression and the defense against regression plays an important part in abnormal drinking. In his book, *Adolescence and the Conflict of Generations,** Dr. Gerald Pearson points out the defense of regression in adolescence as follows:

Adolescence and the Conflict of Generations by GERALD H.J. PEARSON, M.D. New York, W.W. Norton & Co., Inc., 1958, p. 37.

At no other time in the individual's life is the conflict between the wish to be a baby, to be passive and dependent, and the need to be grown up, to be active and independent, so clearly seen. The actions which demonstrate either the wish or the need are repudiations of reality and an attempt to replace it by wish fulfillment almost like the baby's attempts at hallucinatory gratifications. The adolescent frequently shows this conflict by seeming to fluctuate between two poles. Today, he is a "big man" and neither needs nor will take advice or suggestions from anyone. In fact, his feelings are badly hurt if either advice or suggestion is offered. This reaction of hurt feelings is a good indication that the problem is one of inadequate self-esteem. Perhaps the next day or at some time shortly after he is no longer a big man but only a "little baby"—not able to make any decisions or even to do anything for himself, and behaving as if he were totally incapable and extremely dependent.

Of course, this further relinquishment of the testing of reality is another factor in the temporary weakening of the ego. However, both the wish and the need are directed to the environment and thus keep the ego still in contact with reality; therefore a truly psychotic picture seldom develops, although at times some of the reactions appear very close to it.

Let me compare this with the emotional conflicts that are exhibited by many addicted drinkers. The patient without insight does not know that he is overwhelmed by an emotional discomfort similar to that exhibited by the adolescent. The addicted drinker has translated this discomfort into drinking (regressing), and then struggles to curtail his drinking or abstain from it (defense against regression). The abstinent period eventually proves so emotionally uncomfortable that the defense of regression is brought into play by again resorting to alcohol.

In retrospect, I can identify much of my emotional discomfort when I had a drinking problem to the emotional discomfort of the adolescent. For instance, I was dependent on alcohol, though this was the last thing I would have admitted, and when drinking I satisfied passive dependent needs. Sober, I felt the need to be active and independent. When drinking I certainly repudiated reality by alcoholically induced wish-fulfillment. For instance, I might be worried about being in debt, but after enough alcohol the worry disappeared and I would think as follows, as the self-complimentary effect of alcohol had its sway: With my ability, and even genius, the debts would be paid because of masterful and immediate accomplishment in some form of endeavor. Certainly I felt no need for advice, and was hostile to any suggestions, and my feelings were badly hurt if such well-meaning advice or suggestion was offered. My inadequate self-esteem must have been pretty low at this period. On reindulgence in alcohol, I ceased to be the "big man" and became, unconsciously, the little baby not able to make any decisions or do anything for myself. Fortunately, when sober I was able to keep the ego still in contact with reality most of the time.

Successful therapy requires that the patient dare to face and share his discomfort with us. He must gradually dissect and understand this discomfort to the point where he seeks, like the adolescent, to keep his ego more and more in touch with reality.

The following short account given us by a frank patient and a member of his family during an early interview is illustrative of much that has been written in this chapter.

Mr. X. was born of an excellent family of Quaker and Dutch ancestry. There was no history of mental disease and, with the exception of an uncle on his maternal side, no record of abnormal drinking. The grandparents had been successful in business, and his parents were comfortably established with little incentive to further enhance their pecuniary resources. The mother might be described as a typical society woman. She had married the man who was chosen by her parents and approved by her social set. However, in her youth she had fallen in love with a man of whom her family disapproved because, although acceptable and attractive as a potential husband, he was socially unimportant. Like a dutiful daughter, she unwisely acquiesced in her parents' desire and eventually married her family's choice rather than expose herself to their criticism. The result was a humdrum, uninteresting union, and to escape she engaged in all kinds of club work, social service, and philanthropic activities. As her only son grew older, she became more and more solicitous about him, and consequently overprotected him in every way, thus denying him the normal "give and take" of everyday existence.

The father of the patient, on the other hand, was disappointed in the outcome of this marriage, in which there was no real love and little understanding. As time went on, he devoted himself more and more to business and club life, avoiding a home which fell far short of his expectations and ideals. As his son matured, the father endeavored to act as a counterfoil to the pampering attitude of the mother. He felt the boy's disaster was inevitable unless he attempted to compensate by handling the boy in a stern, austere manner. The result of this environment on the child is rather obvious. He found himself "out on a limb," uncertain which way to jump. Being human, he leaped to his mother's arms where he was overprotected, flattered and completely untrained for the battle of life. Although he admired his father, he was terrified by his unnatural sternness and domineering tactics.

When eighteen years of age, the boy entered college, and again found himself "out on a limb," but this time there was no place to jump. He was released from both the solicitous pampering of his mother, and the dominant commands of his father. Mr. X. thus describes his feelings and reaction: "I was torn between a stimulating feeling of independence on the one hand, and insecurity on the other. I found myself totally bewildered by the matter-of-fact manner with which my contemporaries faced the problems of existence. They appeared so capable and unafraid in meeting their everyday problems. I craved their approval and wanted to be considered one of them; but I had no technique with which to establish a friendly relationship.

"I remember my first visit to the village inn and my excitement and relief at discovering that alcohol would dissipate my feelings of insecurity and inferiority to the point where I felt socially secure. In this environment I was accepted by a 'fast' group who were rendered uncritical by their use of alcohol. The inn became a mecca to which I made frequent pilgrimages. Here was afforded, at small expense and no effort, a sense of well-being and importance. While under the influence of a few drinks, I fancied myself an outstanding member of my class; and my drinking companions flattered me by welcoming me into their circle. Even the recital of some drunken prank in which we had all participated made me feel important and pleasantly conspicuous. This zest for recognition soon led to my seeking out bizarre things to do while under the influence of liquor. My drinking companions always applauded. Eventually, in my freshman year, I was called before the dean, who symbolized my father's stern personality. As I recall, he was kindly and gave me good, wholesome advice which was promptly rejected because it was so like my father's guidance.

"When I had to leave college, I returned to a family wherein open warfare had been declared. My father blamed my mother for my failure at college; and my mother accused my father of almost everything imaginable. A position in a bank was secured for me, and I soon discovered that my inferiority feeling, due to my failure at college, could be dissipated by the use of my new found friend, alcohol. The next five years constituted a makeshift escape from unpleasant reality due to the conflict at home, and my resentment against both my mother's overprotection and my father's discipline. I found myself living more and more at the club, and almost entirely preoccupied in a mad search for excitement amidst the social activities offered every young bachelor in a large city. During this period I drank a great deal, but had no realization that I was addicted to, or dependent upon alcohol. I persisted in my endeavor to become conspicuous when under its influence, and soon I found I had a reputation, at first for being very gay; but later I sensed the gossips' whisper, 'Isn't it too bad he drinks so much?'

"At the end of five years, I married. During those first two years of married life, my wife and I devoted ourselves to a whirl of social engagements, most of which seemed to demand that I use alcohol almost continuously. Then our first child was born. My drinking had now become a problem to me and my wife. I was getting a little bit tighter than anybody else at parties. I was beginning to look forward to lunch at the club merely to remedy my shaky hands and 'awfully gone' feeling with a few drinks at the bar. It was not long before I concluded that a morning eye-opener would be advisable in order to brace me sufficiently and tide me over until lunch time.

"At length, because of my alcoholic breath and inefficiency, I was 'hauled on the carpet' in the president's office, where I was warned that it was imperative that I get hold of myself and learn to control my drinking. This frightened me. Like the dean in college before, the president no doubt was the admired and dreaded surrogate of the stern father of my boyhood.

"I tried going 'on the wagon,' and was surprised to learn it was not so difficult to do without alcohol. It was painful, however, to endure the boredom and restlessness caused by abstinence. My drinking companions at the club became rather dull, silly human beings, and I felt excluded from their conversation about drinking escapades. I became petulant and terribly sorry for myself. My home life was very dreary, and my wife's worried attitude concerning my drinking made me guiltily furious. My moroseness had a repercussional effect so that marital life became a 'cat and dog' existence. After two months of abstinence from alcohol, I decided that I could drink in moderation. I was welcomed back into the arms of my drinking companions, and even my wife admitted that things seemed to be going better now that I had 'control of myself.' This semi-normal control lasted four months, during which time I thought I was able to limit my drinking comparatively well. However, at the end of this period, my shaking hands had to be quieted by a heavy drink before breakfast; and the next time I was summoned to the president's office, I was fired.

"Self-pity now became extreme. The hours normally spent at the office were now spent at the club with other men whose working interfered with their drinking. Every evening the return home became more cloudy and vague. At first, I was just tight at dinner. Pretty soon I was dead drunk by that time and had to be assisted to bed. From this time on, a sanitarium was necessary to sober me up. It seems as if I have spent the last five years in sobering up, and then looking forward to the day when I could drink again. I realize that it cannot go on any longer because I am physically, mentally, and morally so far down the ladder that destruction appears inevitable. I am willing and anxious to do anything that will help me, provided you think I can be shown what to do."

The man who gave this account of his life came from an environment where there was a great deal of economic and social security. Let me cite an example where the reverse was true.

This patient came to the Institute from a distant state. His history indicated that he was a successful man in his profession. He said his marriage was pretty shaky and his abnormal drinking was materially affecting his work and his home life. He described his early environment as one of great poverty. His mother had been deserted by her husband when her child was three years of age. She had been a schoolteacher in a depressed rural area prior to her marriage. When her husband deserted her she went back to teaching, and by great personal sacrifice, often denying herself adequate food, she was able to get schooling and later college and postgraduate education for her son. He excelled in his scholastic field, throughout school, college and postgraduate work, as he later excelled in his profession.

As he talked about his childhood and his schooling, it became obvious that he had had no play and no companionship with other children. At college, he could not afford to join a fraternity and he said, "Even if I had been able to afford it, I probably wouldn't have because it might have distracted me from my work." In his case, being head of his class was the be-all and end-all of his mother's and his ambition.

In summing up many hours of mutual exploration of this man's personality, he and I reached the conclusion that play had been completely denied him at all growth levels and now as a successful professional man he could afford to indulge in some play, but always felt ill at ease and guilty when he did so. He soon found in alcohol a way to handle this emotional discomfort, and alcohol became more and more important to him. "In fact," he said, "it has become more important than anything else."

I cite this overly brief history of this patient merely to bring out the contrast in environment as compared to the description of the previous patient. The first patient had too much financial security; the second patient had too little. The thing they had in common was a difficulty in forming an adequate ego in crucial formative years.

All that the brief account of Mr. X.'s case gives is a vague picture of an environment destructive to mature emotional growth, and the patient's own account of how he used alcohol abnormally during the period of adolescence and maturity up to the time he consulted us. The history signified a state of mind so maladjusted in facing reality on a normal basis that the use of alcohol or some other way of eluding reality seemed inevitable. The fact that it was the misuse of alcohol that showed itself as a symptom of maladjustment seems to me not a matter of chance, but due to a lack of ego formation. With greater ego formation, though still incomplete, Mr. X. might have shown other symptoms without the necessity of using alcohol abnormally.

Frequently, following an acute alcoholic episode on the withdrawal from alcohol, we see many transitory neurotic reactions, particularly anxiety states. For instance, during the course of his breakdown, the abnormal drinker may suffer from the following symptoms which seldom appear collectively as neurotic symptoms in a normal drinker: defects of attention, fear of insanity, insomnia, hypochondriacal attitudes, lack of emotional control, headaches, amnesia for periods of intoxication, loss of appetite, tics and, perhaps, the very gesture of drinking reveals its compulsive nature. These symptoms often appear in close succession following abstinence, and the patient's tried and true defense is the old psychic pain killer, alcohol.

This leads me to believe that the abnormal drinker's lack of ego formation differs from that of the neurotic who develops chronic neurotic manifestations. I would say, therefore, that the neurotic has never learned to handle conflict, and the abnormal drinker has found in alcohol a denial of conflict. One way in which I gauge patients' potential for recovery is by the amount of conflict they have about reindulging in alcohol. The patient who does not have conflict about reindulgence is missing a necessary growth struggle.

Even the frank psychoses, or insanities, such as schizophrenia, manic-depressive and paranoid delusional states can show their symptoms in an abnormal drinker. The apathy toward reality as seen in schizophrenia is scarcely more complete than the detachment from reality achieved by the extreme addicted drinker as he sits with a vapid expression, oblivious of his lack of control of bodily functions. In another phase of intoxication, the same patient may show symptoms of a manic-depressive nature with decidedly manic or excited behavior during the initial period of intoxication, followed by a depression or melancholia which sometimes ends in suicide. Many abnormal drinkers sooner or later show signs of a paranoid nature: suspicion, jealousy and ideas of persecution. Sometimes these are so dynamic that they eventuate in murder. When we take into consideration the narcotic effect of alcohol on the inhibiting functions, we are given a glimpse of the Pandora's box of mental abnormality latent in all of us.

The question of whether the abnormal drinking in a given case is a manifestation of underlying mental disease is never to be answered by amateur psychiatry or psychology. Bear in mind that the normal man has periods of introversion and introspection when he is apt to be moody and to appear detached from his immediate environment. Equally, he has periods of slight unreasoning depression and moments of spontaneous elation.

In addicted drinking, these characteristics are exaggerated due to the malfunctioning of the normal inhibiting faculties, and one gets a startling picture of abnormality in extreme intoxication, which might easily lead one to presuppose a grave mental illness. This understandable impulse to diagnose the reason for a man's addicted drinking problem is best left to those who have made an exhaustive study of it.

When the fact that the well-adjusted citizen, whom no one would call neurotic, may inadvertently become intoxicated and exhibit behavior just as abnormal as his less fortunate brother who is classed as a drunkard, is taken into consideration, we can readily see how confusing may be the attempt to analyze addicted drinking symptoms. It may take a trained therapist many months before he gains insight into the basis of an addiction to alcohol. Therefore, well-meaning, but unskilled attempts to supply the answer for abnormal drinking are not likely to be successful or helpful. Truly, this is one of the instances where a bit of knowledge is a dangerous thing.

I believe that the addicted drinker permits the emotional force on an infantile level less painful egress at the higher levels and the narcotic effects of alcohol are resorted to. One then gets a picture of the incentive that causes the psychically maladjusted person to make his painful response to reality less painful by this method. It is, in effect, a struggle on the part of the person with an insufficient development of personality to make himself more comfortable in an adult world.

The fact that alcohol works, and for a time works too well, is responsible for the beginning of an addiction to alcohol. All may go well in the early history of a man who is using alcohol to overcome his feelings of emotional discomfort, but soon the psychological danger point is reached. Then what has heretofore seemed to be a beneficial reaction to alcohol ceases to work in the old satisfactory manner, and the drinker finds that an increased quantity of the anesthetic is necessary to gain the desired results. But these results are like the will-o'-the-wisp in that they seem to be always just out of reach. Perhaps the higher sensitive levels become immune to the former narcotic effect of alcohol, and increased quantities are demanded in order to narcotize the deeper psychic mechanism and to acquire the same end result that was originally gained by moderate intoxication.

When this happens, it seems as if one were deliberately attempting to get drunk. Of course, consciously, the addicted drinker will assure you, his drunken condition came about by chance. Actually, we believe that what happens is that in his search for the pleasurable reactions to alcohol, he is forced to drink such quantities* that the lower nervous functions and all that is contained in the unconscious are affected, so that the normal censor of unconscious, instinctive forces is anesthetized. Still deeper intoxication is resorted to in order to narcotize the outcroppings of the unconscious mind, since they are so incompatible with the civilized, mature conception of self.

Only in the alcoholic psychosis and its concomitant, paranoid delusional states, do we gain a picture of some of the unconscious, self-accusatory complexes that the abnormal drinker has been attempting to "drench" out of recognition. Here, in his last extremity, alcohol has played its devotee false, and in order to save himself from being overwhelmed by self-accusations, it becomes necessary for him to use the device of projection, so that he can accuse the environment

---

*Of course, we do not include in this description an often observed reaction to alcohol, which might be described as a pathological susceptibility, brought on by addicted drinking. Very little alcohol produces startling effects, and we have seen two drinks result in a convulsive seizure. In other words, up to a certain state in addiction, the abnormal drinker is forced to drink large quantities of alcohol in order to gain the desired anesthetic end. As deterioration takes place, which is probably psysical, the quantity of alcohol necessary for this reaction becomes less.

of persecuting him. This phenomenon is pointed out in an old popular song, "You made me what I am today."

It is interesting to note that patients are not able to tell you of the state of mind that they had in deep intoxication. I believe that the regression they obtain is so primitive and infantile that the more mature segment of the personality censors it and will not permit it to reach conscious levels.

In citing the rather extreme reactions that may occur in a person with a drinking problem, I wish to remind the reader that abnormal drinking is an insidious and progressive sick response to addiction to alcohol. By and large, the earlier the patient faces his problem, the more encouraging is the prognosis. Unhappily, the last stages of addicted drinking, where there seems to be a fixed and irremediable deterioration of the personality, are not responsive to the treatment measures outlined in this book.

Chapter VI

THEORY OF TREATMENT

The physician treats a physical disease by identifying it and applying his training to determining the proper treatment. With surgery, drugs, care and the passage of time, he brings the patient to the point where the cause has been removed, the effects overcome and the body healed.

The therapist, treating a maladjustment whose symptom is abnormal dependency on alcohol, has a problem which the physician never has to face. The cause of the disease lies within the patient's personality. The cure must be supplied by the patient to be effective, and the patient tends to armor and protect the cause so that the cure cannot be easily administered. Again, in opposition to some physical disease which is always caused by a specific microorganism, identical from case to case, the cause of addicted drinking lies uniquely in the patient's personality and must be rediscovered in each case, not only by the therapist, but with his help by the patient also. We define the maladjustment by stating that the personality which shows abnormal dependency on alcohol has taken a sick way of adapting to reality, for the addicted drinker has, indeed, adapted or readjusted, but not in the way which is best for himself or for society. This sick adjustment is destroying the personality which, nevertheless, harbors and protects the sick adjustment and surrounds it with rationalizations and defenses.

The next logical step would seem to be to treat the personality so that it will no longer wish to harbor the abnormal dependency on alcohol, but where we attempt this we are apt to run into a stone wall for the reason that the abnormal dependency on alcohol makes it impossible to reach the personality. The disease-causing organism, one might say, is encysted within the personality while its poisons have affected the personality's ability to communicate. How, then, do we reach the personality that harbors the abnormal dependency on alcohol? The answer is that we reach it through the alcoholic conflicts shared with us in therapy by the patient who has voluntarily sought our assistance. As a rule, in the early part of treatment, the patient will undergo a great deal of conflict as to whether or not to drink. As I have pointed out, there is an occasional exception where a patient seems free of conflict after he has terminated his drinking. This is called a flight into recovery.

I have no doubt that the patients believing in their flight into recovery think they are well, but they are really fooling themselves. They leave treatment totally unprepared to meet and understand the inevitable conflict that is bound to arise; and when they do encounter it, they usually resolve it by turning to alcohol again. This flight into recovery is actually a temporary suppression of a sick dependency on alcohol. Actually, the working-out of many years of alcoholic dependency and the adjustment of the personality to acceptance of not drinking is a long, hard role and needs help until the patient has made his not-drinking a part of his personality.

The patient who was and is willing to share the conflicts about drinking that he encounters between meetings with us has taken the first step in accomplishing something very worthwhile and important. How, then, do we bring it about that the patient is willing to discuss his conflicts about alcohol with us? I do this by explaining to the patient that of course he is going to want to drink again after he has reached a state of sobriety, and I explain to the patient that these conflicts are inevitable and to be expected as part of his struggle for recovery. I do not suggest to the patient that he say, "Get thee behind me, oh wicked drinking!" I suggest just the opposite. I encourage him to bring the thought right out and face it, and I also encourage him to question himself as to why he wants a drink at certain times. His first answer to himself will probably be a rationalization. "I'm tired." "I'm nervous." "I'm angry." Or, "I wanted a drink because for many years I was accustomed to taking it at certain times."

No matter how skillful the patient is in rationalizing why he wants a drink, the rationalization is never the real answer. He wants the drink because of a sense of deep emotional discomfort. He believes that a drink will make him more comfortable, and yet he knows that if he takes a drink to make him more comfortable, he will not stop there. He knows, but must learn to believe that this reindulgence in alcohol even in the most moderate quantity will in time lead to heavier and heavier drinking and the inevitable alcoholic episode with all of its distress.

I remember a patient of many years ago in the early part of treatment going to Washington for an important business meeting. While he was in Washington, he relapsed, and he told me that he came home in bad shape. His wife said to him, "Oh, how could you, after you've just started treatment?" He replied, "I don't really know. I just closed my mind." His wife's remark was interesting. She said to him, "What would you say to the children if they gave you the explanation that they just closed their minds?" This patient was intelligent and sincere in his desire to recover, and he brought up the fact that if one closed his mind, he and he alone was responsible for closing it. I explained to him that over the years he had made his abnormal drinking become part of his personality, and that the job of making not-drinking become a part of his personality would take a long while and much conflict until he reached the point where his not-drinking seemed for him natural and acceptable.

Actually, having conflict, daring to face it, and resolving it without turning to alcohol is a very important self-treatment measure which all patients need to undergo. As the patient makes progress in therapy, he is asked to examine why he wanted a drink at the times he mentioned. Because of the treatment he has had, he is no longer able to use rationalization in the way he did before treatment. Then he begins to see that these drink impulses that he encounters are caused by a discomfort within himself, and with the help of therapy he explores the reasons for this discomfort.

Contrary to widely held opinions, this unhappiness and discomfort does not clear up if a person stops drinking. Abstinence does not solve immediately a deficiency in personality formation, but abstinence with good treatment may well help the patient to discover the cause of his unhappiness and discomfort, and so to get at the root of the trouble, and in time to deal with his emotional discomfort and unhappiness in a mature rather than a regressive way. Filling a deficiency is an emotional growth struggle, and it is not going to take place over night.

There is an old axiom based on the primitive man: "A threat produces one of two responses: fight or flee." We either wish to run away from it, or we motivate anger and try to destroy the thing that is threatening us. For the animal these two alternatives seem blissfully simple, but a human being from earliest childhood onward is told that it is wrong to kill and cowardly to run away. Man, with his veneer of civilization, knows that he cannot give vent to his primitive self. If he kills his enemy, he will probably be hanged. If he runs away, he will be branded a coward. The addicted drinker, without being aware of it, is indulging in very primitive acting out of such a dilemma. He is running away, and he is killing. In his case, it happens to be himself that he is running away from, and himself that he is killing; thus, the enemy that is threatening him lies within himself. He is burning down the church in order to get rid of the bats in the belfry. It is hoped that modern treatment can help exterminate the bats in a way that is far less destructive and wasteful.

What are the bats in the belfry? What are the inner conflicts that prove to be so great that the patient wishes to run away from himself and eventually to destroy himself? I am sure it would be a great relief to the reader and a source of satisfaction to me if I could give an answer that would fit all patients, but, as I have pointed out in the first part of this chapter, we are dealing with individual personalities, and each person's reason for addicted drinking will be individual and unique.

We know that from infancy to maturity the child goes through a terrifically speeded-up evolutionary process. The infant is primitive. His first love is himself. Very slowly, he dares to project his love on to his parents or his brothers and sisters, and very early he learns that this projected love, if it is frustrated, can turn into anger and hatred so that the child is in conflict with its emotions from a very early age onward. These are the emotional growing pains that are necessary in order to develop into a mature human being, and if the child is fortunate it accepts these growing conflicts, deals with them, and because of this emerges as an adult able to deal with the conflicts of living with a fair degree of stability and maturity.

But what if these conflicts in childhood are never resolved or faced? Then we have the phenomenon of a "mature" man or woman unable to face and resolve the normal conflicts of adulthood. It is as if the adult takes his cue from the unresolved or unfaced conflicts of childhood, and is therefore unable to face the mature conflicts of adulthood.

Psychiatry teaches us that there are a great many sick manifestations of the adult unable to deal with his conflicts. We are concerned in this book with the problem of addicted drinking, and here we see the great compromiser, alcohol, entering the picture. The drug, alcohol, is resorted to in order to escape discomfort, and the insidious part of it is that in the early stages of drinking, alcohol works and works too well. But as for any pain killer, the patient gets habituated to it, and as time progresses it takes more and more pain killer to alleviate the pain; and where in the early stages a few drinks did the trick, as the addiction to alcohol progresses, it takes deeper intoxication to alleviate the discomfort that the patient is running away from.

The patient, being aware that he is using alcohol in an abnormal way, has his conflict increased because of a sense of shame, futility and remorse. The initial personality discomfort that may have been dispelled or avoided by alcohol in the early stages is now far worse because of his abnormal dependency on alcohol. Without being aware of it, the patient is like the man whose car is on fire and who reaches for a bucket and throws the contents on the fire. It happens to be a bucket of alcohol. He is using the wrong quencher to put out the fire; in fact, he is rekindling a fire that might have burnt itself out without his excited endeavor to help.

When the patient has relinquished alcohol and dares search backward to the initial growth steps that were incomplete in childhood, we see why he drank abnormally. I remember discussing with the father of one patient his son's difficulty in adjusting and the treatment I felt was indicated in order to help him. With great hesitancy and embarrassment, the father brought up the fact that his wife, a socially prominent woman from another city, had not wanted this child and had taken a patent medicine purported to cause abortion. This had not worked, and the child was born physically healthy. Our psychological department who tested this patient found no indication of brain damage. The father's remark is interesting. He said, "Could it possibly be that the medication my wife took in the early part of pregnancy could have caused this abnormal behavior in my son?" There was no indication that the medicine had done any harm or any good, but the important aspect which was completely missed by the father was that the mother had not wished to have this child, and the patient even as an infant in the crib started to sense and feel this rejection.

I hope that this chapter conveys to the reader the understanding that abnormal drinking is a symptom of a maladjustment of the personality that began years before the symptom itself appeared. Keeping in mind that we are dealing with a chronic illness of the personality, we realize that suppression of the surface symptom, abnormal drinking alone, means curing the effect rather than finding and curing the cause. One patient expressed this very well to me. Early in treatment he said, "Giving up alcohol seems like a negative gesture rather than a positive gesture." Later in treatment he was able to comprehend that readjusting his personality with insight was, in truth, a positive approach to forming an adequate, mature personality which his drinking symptoms would frustrate.

In reading over this "Theory of Treatment," a nursery rhyme came to mind:

> Little Jack Horner sat in the corner,
> Eating a Christmas pie!
> He put in his thumb, and pulled out a plum,
> And said, "What a good boy am I!"

In condensing case histories and arriving at conclusions acceptable to patient and therapist, the countless hours of struggle on the patient's part to gain insight must for brevity's sake be left out. We who are trying to help do not have "Jack Horner's" pride in pulling out the plum. We realize full well that the patient is the one who struggled to gain insight and had the courage to face the raw wounds to his personality that were so painful that he turned to a self-destructive medium in order to escape the pain of his maladjustment.

There is no question in my mind that some psychiatrists will disagree with this brief outline of theory of treatment. They will reason that since abnormal drinking is a symptom of deeper psychopathology, one must go to the root of the psychopathology and the symptom, abnormal drinking, will then be discarded by the patient. My approach is that you can best help the patient to reach insight into the psychopathology by having him share his symptoms, i.e., his need for abnormal drinking, with you. When he asks for help in discarding the symptom which is destroying him, he runs into inevitable discomfort created by his relinquishing alcohol. As he dares to feel this discomfort the chance of the patient's analyzing it becomes greater and the patient will gradually see that after he has relinquished alcohol he is running into emotional discomfort, and that these emotional discomforts can, by being shared with us, lead to a great deal of understanding as to why he resorted to abnormal drinking as an emotional pain killer.

In summation of the theory of this treatment plan, I believe we can say, first, that it requires an active approach on the part of the patient. From the first interview throughout treatment, the patient is given to understand that he solves his problem, not by passively submitting to treatment, but by realizing that he has a difficult job ahead of him. The patient who asks for help realizes that something has been taken away by his voluntarily relinquishing alcohol. This leaves him with his dependency needs all dressed up with no place to go, but he soon finds his dependency needs are being transferred to the therapist. This can be a crucial moment in treatment for both the patient and us. If properly handled, the patient becomes aware that our role is like that of the teacher who teaches methods and guides the student to understanding, but who does not give out answers or solve problems. The teacher helps the student by showing him the structure of the problem and introducing him to the use of problem-solving tools, but the student is successful only if he solves his own problem.

Chapter VII

APPROACH TO TREATMENT

In our approach to patients, we frankly express the belief that they have two problems, first, an addiction to alcohol which will lead to their destruction, and second, a maladjustment in their personality which led to their unconsciously seeking this escape. We point out that psychotherapy must be a joint effort by patient and therapist to gain understanding of the patient's personality makeup and all the environmental factors going far back into his childhood. We explain the desirability of a cooperative inventory of the factors that led, first, to the need for escape from reality by way of alcohol, and second, to the state of mind that could find escape only in the toxic effect of alcohol.

The keystone of the arch which supports the personality of each patient does not fit properly. Therapist and patient are jointly working toward a firmer readjustment of this keystone.

I tell the patient that his abnormal drinking is a symptom of the unfinished business of developing an adequate personality. The fact that he took to abnormal drinking in a blind attempt to fill the deficient areas in ego formation and suffered a good deal of misery and social condemnation in no way changes the scientific aspect of his condition. His condition is placed in the same category as hysterical blindness, or

95

a neurasthenic sensation of heart pain or any other symptom of psychoneurotic disorder which escapes social condemnation.

This seems to us to be the only fair and honest attitude. It puts the treatment of abnormal drinking on the best basis and leaves the patient in no doubt as to where he stands. The intelligent patient will soon realize that our attitude is not disapproving, since we are dealing with the illness along the lines of treatment that would be applied to other emotional maladjustments. This point, though it may seem trivial, is nevertheless important because addicted drinkers are so often super-sensitive about the stigma attached to their problem. If they sense a disapproving attitude or a disciplinary approach, they will retire into a smoke screen of resistance that will statically resist any method of exploration, suggestion, or treatment.

With the full realization that no two personalities are exactly alike, our approach to and treatment of each patient must, of necessity, be flexible enough to permit considerable variation. Patients are seen from all economic, social and educational levels, and we realize that no set A, B, C treatment plan would be universally applicable. The particular variation selected depends upon the analysis of each personality as it reveals itself to us. With this in mind, the reader will appreciate that our description of treatment is based on the observation of a large group of patients; their response to treatment; their resistance against getting well as opposed to their desire to be cured; their suggestibility, and their potentialities of leading happy, nondrinking lives.

Since the bulk of patients are referred to us by men in the practice of medicine, medical specialists, or recovered patients, psychological treatment may be said to have started before the patient actually consults us, in the sense that the suggestion that he can be helped has already been implanted by someone whom he admires and respects. The fact that an individual does come to us for consultation about his drinking is a partial recognition on his part that he needs help. He therefore comes with a psychological beginning already made in the direction of adjustment.

In my early years of dealing with people with a drinking problem, it was rather generally thought that legal commitment was a necessary measure to protect the addicted drinker. We have since found that this is not a solution or even a desirable method in the majority of cases. Legal commitment may be a necessary safeguarding measure in certain instances. However, custodial care should not be insisted upon until every aspect of the condition has been analyzed. Generally speaking, it is only advisable when all parties concerned are convinced that the possibilities of obtaining cooperation from the patient are nil, or when the abnormalities of behavior are so dangerous that no other method of handling the situation is feasible. The danger inherent in commitment is that the individual often becomes unconsciously dependent upon the authority that placed him in an institution. This dependency is very apt to be coupled with a feeling of resentment that precludes effectiveness of a reeducational plan of treatment.

Because our work has to do solely with those who seek our help, and are anxious to do something about their addiction problem, we deal with the most favorable group of addicted drinkers, and our suggestions as to treatment can be far more flexible because of the very spirit of those who consult us. The majority of patients usually need a time away from their customary environment, where they can get into better physical and nervous shape, and frequently their willingness to accept the protection of a hospital during the early stages of getting well is a manifestation of the fact that they are sincere and wish to cooperate to the utmost. This decision, however, is left to the patient, and if he thinks he can undertake treatment without the necessity of going to a hospital, we are perfectly willing for him to try. If he finds he cannot make a go of it in his own environment, it is understood that he will be perfectly frank about it and accept the facilities afforded him at a hospital.

Allowing the patient to make his own decision about going to a hospital does away with the resentment that might be brought about by an overpersuasive technique. Many of our patients have tried to make their nonalcoholic adjustment without the help of a hospital and have failed. They have proved to their own satisfaction that they need it. The fact that many other patients have been able to give up alcohol in their own environment, without the necessity of hospitalization, is evidence against an arbitrary attitude. If it is necessary for the patient to go to a hospital, this part of treatment should be considered by him and the staff of the hospital as a preliminary to outpatient interviews, rather than as an end in itself.

The fact that most of our patients undertake treatment in an open hospital implies to the patient that we are treating them as adults in need of help rather than as children who need to be punished by being locked up. The fact that the patients know they can leave the hospital at any time they choose puts the burden of responsibility on them, and patients usually appreciate this. Of course, there are patients who are too sick to be able to cooperate in an open hospital. They soon reveal this by going out and drinking. We do not censure them for this, but we do tell them that they are wasting their time and their money by their lack of cooperation. The choice is always given them to go to a closed section of the hospital until they feel they can approach treatment on a more adult level.

This book concerns itself chiefly with the psychological and reeducational aspects of abnormal drinking, but we do not minimize the importance of physical complications and the need for repairing tissue damage traceable to alcohol and for bringing the patient up to his physical optimum. The hospital and sanatorium fulfill an important function in this aspect of the treatment of addiction to alcohol. We do not believe, however, that addicted drinkers are cured by being made sound and well in their bodies alone, and the hospital, while it may be the means to an end, is not the end itself.

We suggest to our patients that they try to be perfectly frank with their friends about their reasons for giving up alcohol. Their friends have, in all probability, been thinking for a long while that it would be a very good thing if they did give up drinking. However, many addicted drinkers choose to think that no one realizes the abnormality of their condition. In most instances where patients have seen the wisdom of being frank, the results have been good. When the patient feels secure enough to go on record with his friends and with himself as having realized the true seriousness of his problem, he has proved to himself and to others that he is facing the issue in a mature way.

As the reader will have gathered, I am against the use of the term *alcoholic,* and I suggest to patients that they do not use this term in describing their problem. If the patient is asked why he does not drink, it is far better for him to say, "I stopped drinking because alcohol played hell with my nerves." Such a statement indicates a mature decision based on mature reasoning, and conveys to a friend or acquaintance that his reason for not drinking is not because he was threatened by divorce or the loss of a job, but because he has made the decision on his own. On the other hand, should he say, "I stopped drinking because I am an alcoholic," those people in his environment, being uncertain of the meaning of the term may well interpret it as a stigma or weakness, and hence try to shield or protect the patient or feel responsible for him. They are apt to reason, "If he is an alcoholic, should I serve drinks when he is around?" It is true that the statement, "I don't drink because alcohol played hell with my nerves" is not very scientific; however, it conveys in lay language a reasonable summation of why a man or woman chooses not to drink.

An intelligent man or woman who has once recognized his serious problem with drinking is facing his problem, perhaps for the first time, with common sense. I do not advocate patients making a production out of the fact that they have had a serious problem with alcohol, and at long last have had sense enough to face it. In time, their friends and acquaintances will accept the fact that these patients have relinquished alcohol, and therefore the patients should have increased self-respect, as well as the respect of their friends and relatives. One who presents himself as having given up drinking for his own good, and having taken on not-drinking as a natural way to face reality, will in due course impress this attitude on society. One who attempts to hide an addiction problem is deceiving no one, himself included, and if he persists in pretending that nothing is wrong despite the evidence, he is obviously making his readjustment more difficult.

We certainly do not urge our patients to declare to the world that they are giving up alcohol, but we do point out to them that after a reasonable time has elapsed and they are assured that the treatment and the reeducational measures are proving effective, it is then advisable for them to be perfectly frank. We do not urge it, but merely point out to them that most people who get well have in time been willing to burn their bridges in the matter of being frank about their problem.

We have never seen anyone lose prestige by the admission that he had a serious problem with alcohol. Friends will respect such a statement as a return to sanity. On the other hand, we have seen even dissipated friends of addicted drinkers treat them with contemptuous tolerance when they pretend that they are only social drinkers.

There is no greater bore than the so-called reformed

drunkard who must tell everybody about his evil existence and way of life while drinking, and "look at me now, Simon-pure." The next step in such a faulty approach is, "I am better than you are because I overcame a problem. You have never had a problem to overcome."

James Thurber, with his masterly understanding of our weaknesses, summed up a certain type of reformed drunkard in the following delightful sketch.

THE BEAR WHO LET IT ALONE*

In the woods of the Far West there once lived a brown bear who could take it or let it alone. He would go into a bar where they sold mead, a fermented drink made of honey, and he would have just two drinks. Then he would put some money on the bar and say, "See what the bears in the back room will have," and he would go home. But finally he took to drinking by himself most of the day. He would reel home at night, kick over the umbrella stand, knock down the bridge lamps, and ram his elbows through the windows. Then he would collapse on the floor and lie there until he went to sleep. His wife was greatly distressed and his children were very frightened.

At length the bear saw the error of his ways and began to reform. In the end he became a famous teetotaller and a persistent temperance lecturer. He would tell everybody that came to his house about the awful effects of drink, and he would boast about how strong and well he had become since he gave up touching the stuff. To demonstrate this, he would stand on his head and on his hands and he would turn cartwheels in the house, kicking over the umbrella stand, knocking down the bridge lamps, and ramming his elbows through the windows. Then he would lie down on the floor, tired by his healthful exercise, and go to sleep. His wife was greatly distressed and his children were very frightened.

Moral: You might as well fall flat on your face as lean over too far backward.

*From *Fables For Our Time,* published by Harper and Row. Originally printed in *The New Yorker.* ©1940 JAMES THURBER.

What is the attitude of the patient who has just started to accept his readjustment to life on a nondrinking basis going to be toward his family? Obviously, because of different personality makeup, each patient will have a different attitude, but generally speaking, we can expect that he will go through quite a long period of time when he is sensitive, rather touchy and in many cases, extremely irritable with those in his immediate family group. Because he has sold himself the idea of a nondrinking approach to reality, he is apt to resent any doubt on the part of his wife or others that his nondrinking approach is on a permanent basis.

The momentum of the determination in many patients seems to sweep away the memory of the trials and tribulations that wives, husbands, mothers and fathers have been under for a period of years. They forget the memory of promises that could never have been kept, and of declarations about the future which were never followed. For this reason, it is well to remind patients that it seems only reasonable to expect a certain amount of insecurity and even suspicion on the part of their families. We ask them to project themselves into the logical position of the family so that they may realize that, were the position reversed, they would in all probabillty take a similar stand.

The more secure a patient becomes in his faith of recovery, the less disturbed he will be by unjust suspicions or even accusations. It may be very annoying to have your wife greet you every evening by a combination of a kiss and a sniff, but this annoyance will disappear with understanding and assurance, and eventually she will forget to sniff. I have also observed the reverse attitude; namely, a wife who is so overjoyed at her husband's facing his problem that after he has had a few interviews or a brief period of hospitalization, she will imply that he is completely recovered. Actually, the patient has a long, hard readjustment road ahead.

Sometimes we observe wives or husbands of our patients

acting in a very immature manner. This may happen in those who marry inebriate lovers with the idea that they will reform them and reshape them to a pattern that will suit their narcissistic tendencies. When they fail, part of their resentment arises from a sense of hurt pride which may show itself childishly in resentment toward treatment because it has been able to bring about the readjustment which they have failed to accomplish.

The truth is that outside of a closed hospital it is absolutely impossible for one individual to prevent another individual from drinking. There is really very little the family can do toward helping the patient.

The wife of a patient with a severe drinking problem made this significant remark to me. "My husband is very intelligent and able in his field, but because of his abnormal drinking he can't hold a position any more and his behavior in the home is upsetting our whole life. I don't see why he is so stupid as to go on drinking."

Of course, this woman was bewildered by the paradox of an intelligent man destroying his right to live a normal life as are all other husbands and wives and friends of those with an addiction to alcohol. This wife would have been just as confused if her husband had a nervous or mental breakdown. My associates in psychiatry inform me that they frequently hear similar statements from wives and husbands of men and women in the first stages of grave mental illness. There are the same expressions of bewilderment and bafflement and the words are almost identical. "My husband is very intelligent and able in his field, but because of his depressed attitude (detachment, confusion, excitement, or abnormal suspicion), he can't hold a position, and his behavior in the home is upsetting our whole life. I don't see why he is so stupid as to go on in this way."

Because these mental symptoms can occur without drinking, it is perhaps easier for the psychiatrist to convince the wife or husband of the neurotic or psychotic patient that his or her partner is mentally sick, and that mental illness, like grave physical illness, must be treated by physicians. Actually, the addicted drinker may be just as sick mentally as the psychotic or psychoneurotic patient. Therefore, the advice to friends and relatives of the patient with a drinking problem should be as follows: Recognize that you are dealing with someone who is off balance in his attitude toward alcohol. Try to understand that he does not deliberately want to destroy his marriage, his job, or his friendships, but that because he is sick in the emotional segment of his mind, he is incapable of coping with his addiction without help.

Once the family and friends of the patient with a drinking problem have recognized that addiction to alcohol is out of the patient's control, they are next faced with the dilemma of what to do about it. First, in all probability the attitude of the man with an addiction to alcohol is such that he cannot see the necessity of seeking psychiatric diagnosis and help. He says, "Oh, I'll be all right. Tomorrow I'll cut down, or next week I'll get off the stuff entirely." Or he may even go "on the wagon" for a while, and then slip off just when his family and friends begin to be encouraged.

Outside of legal commitment, seldom recommended except in grave crises and only after careful psychiatric advice, there is little that can be done with the addicted drinker to get him started in the right direction other than using persuasion. Not bullying or threatening or cajolery, but frank and tactful persuasion. For instance, the wife says to her husband, "Modern psychiatry understands addiction to alcohol as a symptom of emotional illness. I know you have tried to deal with your problem, and just haven't been able to make a go of it. Why not consult someone for understanding and help? At least get a skilled opinion."

Another suggested approach, which is perhaps the best in leading the addicted drinker to a point of asking for help, is to have him read a suitable book on the subject. One of the reasons for writing this book is to have an up-to-date text for this purpose. Careful reading by the patient may have the desired effect of permitting him to identify himself with his addiction problem, to see the threat that alcohol is to his personality, and to seek help just as he would if he recognized the threat of dangerous disease to his body.

As I have mentioned before in this book, I avoid the term *alcoholic* because it means something different to practically everybody who uses it and, unhappily, it carries the connotation of a stigma. If a prospective patient has carefully read the text of this book, it should dissipate any idea that we who might help him consider an addiction to alcohol as a stigma.

One of the most important helpful attitudes of friends and relatives in their effort to understand the problem is to realize that the groundwork of addiction to alcohol was often laid in early childhood and was not within the addicted drinker's control. As I have pointed out, the unresolved formation of the ego in childhood which was carried on into maturity creates a need in the patient to use alcohol for both its tranquilizing and narcotic effect. A better understanding of the problem will often help dispel the doubts so often expressed to us by wives and husbands of addicted drinkers. They question themselves as follows: "Is it my fault that my husband (or wife) became an abnormal drinker? Am I to blame?" Generally speaking, the answer is no, because the maladjustment that made addiction to alcohol possible in all probability started long before the marriage. Though the addicted drinker may, and often does when intoxicated, lay the blame at the door of the marriage partner, it is usually the case that they had little to do with the real cause of their partner's attempt to escape reality by the use of alcohol.

It is understandable that sometimes the harassed wives or

husbands of addicted drinkers have lost all perspective through having been subjected to long periods of embarrassment, annoyance and humilation. This emotional harassment may develop an anxiety state that may persist long after the original cause has disappeared. Not infrequently, the partner of the addicted drinker is just as much in need of treatment as the patient. The factors that may contribute to a neurotic condition in the addicted drinker's husband or wife are so serious and so contrary to mental hygiene that it is often wise for him or her to seek help. Interviews with an understanding psychiatrist may do much to help the drinker's spouse to face the readjustment period as well as to correct the perspective to a degree which will enhance the chance of the patient's recovery.

We ask those who are personally interested in the addicted drinker to accept our findings that in all cases there is ego deficiency. Basically, the drinker lacks the adult ability to face the problems of life. Alcohol gives him, at first, an easy escape from reality. It is often a relief to friends and relatives of the addicted drinker to realize that addiction to alcohol is a product of maladjustment in childhood which created a faulty emotional attitude toward mature reality. This understanding, in turn, will acquaint them with the magnitude of the readjustment project that lies ahead. They will, perhaps for the first time, understand that the problem is not one of just giving up drinking, but of giving up drinking in order to get at the faulty emotional attitudes and change them. It is always a shock to the patient when he reaches the point where he sees how much readjustment lies ahead of him after he has stopped drinking. We want the friends and relatives to know this, and to realize that emotional growth, like physical growth is slow and almost imperceptible when observed from a week-by-week point of view.

It is understandable that occasionally cooperation from the families of patients is difficult to secure. Usually, the members of the family have been consciously, as well as unconsciously, protecting the addicted drinker for many years. It has become a habit. To expect them to change their attitude at once, and to realize that this time the patient is actually doing something mature about his problem is more than can be reasonably expected at the beginning of treatment. However, many intelligent parents, wives, or husbands of our patients have shown remarkable self-control in following a policy of strict noninterference, and in succeeding in refraining from "protective" methods. The cooperation of these wise relatives who understand the psychology of treatment is extremely valuable.

Frequently, we are asked by relatives whether or not they should change the environment, perhaps move to another section of the country in order to make the readjustment easier. The answer is "No." Suggestion to drink lies everywhere in our society, and there is no place where a patient is free of its influence. The important aspect in treatment is to help the patient to develop a secure enough personality so that suggestions that might have influenced him in the past are no longer interesting to him in the present.

Most addicted drinkers live in an environment where alcohol is considered a social accessory. It seems wise that the patient, his family, and friends should understand that he should have the right to offer his friends alcoholic drinks if he wishes. In other words, it is never suggested that the addicted drinker run away from the mass of alcoholic suggestion to which he is continuously subjected. He knows full well that alcohol is easy to get if he wants it. Therefore, surface gestures about abstinence are discouraged, and the family and friends are asked to avoid dramatic gestures such as banishing liquor from the home, and avoiding all parties where alcohol might be served. The burden of decision concerning these matters must rest with the patient. If, at first, he considers not having alcohol in the house, or avoiding parties where drinks are freely served, as common sense self-protection, he should have his own way about such avoidance. Later, if he believes it is safe and he feels secure, he will probably want to attend social occasions where alcohol is served, and he may want to offer his friends drinks. When he has built up this security, he should be able to do this without exciting criticism from his family and friends. It is the problem of the person with an addiction to alcohol, and his way of working out of it, and even if the family and friends do not approve in theory, they should avoid interfering in practice. The chief hope for forming an adequate ego in the addicted drinker is an appeal to the remnants of his maturity; grown-up people must make their own decisions.

Because his drinking was not just a pleasant social custom, but a very sick way of running away from his emotional discomfort, the recovering patient is of necessity very insecure and overly self-conscious about his abstinence. Frequently, his relatives and friends are equally self-conscious and openly or obliquely express this, as well as expressing their anxiety about him.

One patient told me of the following incident after returning to his home city following several months of abstinence, during which time he was under treatment. In this case, his intimate friends knew of his problem, and that he had had treatment. He said, "Shortly after I returned home, my wife and I were asked to a friend's dinner party to which we went, and cocktails were served by the hostess. When she came to me, she said, 'Of course, you won't have any.' I can't tell you how much this annoyed me, and because I knew my host and hostess well, I made an immediate issue of their attitude toward me, by saying to my hostess, 'Mary, that approach was all wrong. Try it over again. Offer the cocktails, and when you come to me, say, "Won't you have one?" and I'll say, "No." At least, give me the privilege of refusing.' "

This patient took a very intelligent, growth-producing step in that he had the courage to present himself securely in his nondrinking readjustment, and at the same time helped his friends in showing them how to adapt themselves to his nondrinking.

If a patient should start drinking again, we ask the family and friends to take their cue from our own attitude, which is as follows: The patient has had a long, chronic illness, probably of many years' duration; therefore, we look on the drinking as a relapse similar to a hemorrhage that might occur in recovery from tuberculosis. In both cases, the relapse is a grave symptom and must be dealt with immediately, and the cause must be unearthed. Sometimes, recurrence of a relapse points out to the patient how very insecure he really is, and impresses on him the necessity of "making haste" in recovery slowly. Whether a relapse occurs or not, we find that it is always difficult for the patient to understand how much personality readjustment lies ahead of him after he has stopped drinking. Overconfidence is a definite danger signal during this period of convalescence.

The convalescent period can be broadly considered to last for five years. By this we mean that during this period the successful patient is changing his emotional attitude through insight and readaptation and is experiencing a gradual degree of maturity that he is learning to appreciate. During this period, the family and friends are asked not to coddle or protect the patient, but to leave the responsibility of treatment up to him with the full realization that we do not cure him, but merely show him how to apply treatment and insight to himself. Therefore, the best overall attitude for friends and relatives to have is to respect the patient for having the courage to face his problem, and the intelligence to apply enlightened self-treatment to that problem. Such an attitude is only workable and applicable to people who are under treatment and really determined to face and solve their problem. Until this point, the family and those of us who wish to help professionally are up against a stone wall.

Another attitude—which is very understandable—of persons who have been married to an addicted drinker over a period of years is that they have acquired, of necessity, the habit of running the household as though it contained an invalid. The same uncertainty motivates them that motivates those in charge of invalids who are apt to become suddenly worse or have attacks which put great responsibility on them and disorganize the household. The addicted drinker's husband or wife has learned through experience to rise to all sorts of untoward situations. They are tuned up to a perpetual state of fear, dissatisfaction and unpleasant excitement, but still, it is excitement. All in all, it might be said that they are running the house of an invalid with all of the uncertainty that that implies. The ringing of the telephone becomes an ominous sound, a possible herald of an accident or some escapade that has run counter to the law. If the telephone does not ring, it is still ominous for the wealth of imaginative drunken pictures contained in its silence. We have seen this state of affairs over and over again, and realize that the abnormal drinker's husband or wife lives in an emotionally charged situation that is bad for them and those dependent on them.

Strangely enough, the wife who has been praying that the patient would overcome his addiction finds herself at a loss as to how to cope with the newly maturing husband who is taking his rightful place in the environment. Keyed up to the abnormalities brought about by the drunken condition of the patient, she is now still keyed up with nothing to be keyed up about. A recent song with the title, "I Can't Get Adjusted to the You Who Got Adjusted to Me" indicates awareness of this problem. Probably deep in the unconscious, some neurotic need has been gratified by the dependency caused by the regressive behavior of the spouse, and this tendency is somewhat frustrated by recovery. Another aspect of their situation is that the wife or husband of an addicted drinker must of necessity be in command of their home life, and though their job is envied by none, and causes them extreme unhappiness, the readjustment of the patient may challenge their sense of importance.

For this and sundry other reasons, it seems like common sense that the spouse of a person with an addiction to alcohol should also have some psychiatric guidance to aid them in understanding their own reactions to the recovery of the husband or wife. Amazingly enough, in our case records we have both men and women who have started drinking to excess after the abnormal drinking spouse was well on the road to recovery. This would seem to signify an attitude of unconscious resentment on their part; i.e., "You have put us through hell for all these years; now we would like you to get a taste of your own medicine," or it may be an unconscious rebellion toward the recovery of husband or wife. Various situations of this sort may arise, and my psychiatric associate and I must be prepared for them although a helpful, cooperative and intelligent attitude is taken by most men and women under these circumstances and is of the greatest benefit to the patient.

Where cooperation can be expected, the family is consulted. As may be gathered, full cooperation from the families of patients is sometimes difficult to secure. Usually, the members of the family have been consciously as well as unconsciously protecting the drinker for many years. That they will change their attitudes and realize that this time the patient is actually doing something about solving his problem in a mature manner is more than we can reasonably expect at the beginning of treatment. However, many intelligent parents, wives, or husbands of our patients have shown remarkable self-control in following a policy of strict noninterference, and have succeeded in refraining from protective methods once they understood the treatment psychology. The cooperation of these wise relatives can be extremely valuable.

Since we avoid the type of persuasion which attempts to make the patient forego his habit by forewarnings of an early alcoholic death, or by pointing to the ethical aspects of his condition, we request the family to do likewise. After all, the patient knows all about the risks and losses his condition has brought about, and in all probability these obvious facts have been brought to his attention many times without effecting any improvement. Therefore, we suggest to the family that this type of approach be avoided. It is our belief that the greatest care must be used in the treatment of the addicted drinker to avoid the old-fashioned, so-called emotional approach to the problem. It is scarcely consistent to ask patients to take a more mature viewpoint concerning their drinking, and at the same time cajole or threaten them as though they were badly behaved children, or put them periodically on an emotional gridiron.

Often, relatives of patients have told us that they have carefully and thoughtfully talked to their inebriate husbands or wives about the obvious consequences of their drinking. They tell us that their well-meaning talks have been met by an apparent understanding, and often by weepy declarations from the patient that he or she will do wrong no more. The response to these well-meaning lectures often gives a false impression that great good has come from them. Usually, all that is accomplished is an increase in the nervous instability that makes the drinker go out and get drunk in earnest, thus increasing the bewilderment and resentment of those who would like to help. The mechanism of this maldiversion of well-intentioned efforts is that the patient is overwhelmed by self-pity. He says to himself, "Oh, how could I have been so weak? How I have hurt myself in the eyes of my fellowman! How unbearable I have made life for my wife and children. I'm killing my mother and father. Look at the way I have dissipated all of my heritage. This is bad indeed. I can't stand it." So rationalizing, he reaches for the usual medium of oblivion, and the tears of remorse are soon well-diluted with alcohol.

Another understandable but futile approach on the part of husbands or wives is the plea, "Won't you give up alcohol for me, or for the children's sake?" Temporarily, such a plea might have some effect, but because the problem is really not understood by the patient, these periods of cessation from drinking for the sake of someone else are short-lived.

Because I have observed this type of reaction in patients so often, I stress very strongly that the patient avoid the idea that he is relinquishing alcohol for the sake of someone else. Well-meaning as such an attitude may seem to be, I point out that the patient is really using someone else as a crutch to enable him to give up alcohol. Unhappily, all such crutches break down eventually.

The same is true of promises. When you promise somebody something, you are sharing the responsibility with the person to whom you made the promise. If the patient thus projects the reasons for his struggle for recovery onto his wife, and then has a Mr.-and-Mrs. argument in which he thinks his wife is unjust or extremely unreasonable, he becomes angry, and the next step is reasoning something like this: "Well, I have made this big sacrifice in giving up alcohol for you, and you are behaving in a hostile and unreasonable way. I am certainly not going to continue to make this sacrifice of giving up alcohol for such an unreasonable woman." And so the patient pours himself a drink.

The deliverers of lectures and talks to addicted drinkers along the lines of, "Look what this is leading you to," and "You're too fine a man or woman to destroy yourself by alcohol," should realize that they have no right to show resentment when their efforts result in failure, because they have witnessed an exaggeration of the emotional instability of the patient, as a result of the fervent emotional pleas. Bullying tactics are equally as futile in the hands of families of patients as they are in the hands of the therapist. When such tactics are analyzed one sees that they gratify certain tendencies in the person with an addiction to alcohol; namely they further motivate and strengthen his disinclination to take the initiative about his problem. For instance, an older brother will order the inebriate patient to do this or that. At once, the brother with an addiction problem rationalizes as follows: "If you are running me, why should I attempt to run myself?" Also, "If you are running me, and I start drinking, then it's your fault and not mine that I drink." The consequence of such tactics is inevitable failure coupled with a sense of unconscious gratification on the part of the patient.

There is an office near me that is occupied by a world-famous neurologist. One day, I stopped him in the hall and said, "It's your duty to tell your patients who have drinking problems, where there is observable neurological damage, of the consequences of their drinking," and he said this was true. I then asked, "Have you ever seen anyone frightened out of his drinking because of what you have told him?" His reply was "Never."

Whenever it is possible to get the cooperation of those most interested in the addicted drinker, we endeavor to explain our point of view and the reasons for requesting noninterference during the patient's convalescence.

Several years ago, I read in a popular magazine an article by a physician who himself had had a drinking problem. The meat of this article was how society should behave toward the addicted drinker who had stopped drinking. This approach frankly made me shudder. Why should society behave in any way in particular to a person because he had

had a drinking problem? Society's job is not to protect or to shield or to avoid suggestion that might influence the patient. Actually, my guess is that a recovered patient would resent this and would hate feeling that he was being protected. Men and women who have had the courage to face and solve an abnormal drinking problem are demonstrably no weaklings and society should not treat them as such.

Chapter VIII

TREATMENT

In this chapter on treatment, I shall describe only my own role in dual therapy. Most of my cases are handled in conjunction with psychiatric associates, but there are exceptions where a patient who is referred by a physician refuses to see a psychiatrist. In these cases, I must carry the entire load of the reeducational treatment, and the medical aspect of the problem is taken care of by the referring physician. Such a situation is not ideal and, though I have been able to help some patients face and solve their addiction problem, I think they would have gained much more by availing themselves of psychiatric help. I have had other paitents who at first refused psychiatric help, but later in treatment realized their need for deeper insight and asked for it.

I think it is important to attempt to describe my own feelings toward a person who comes to me and asks for my help. In the first place, I am completely uncritical of patients with addiction problems because I know that they are in the throes of something they do not understand and I know that they certainly did not deliberately set out to become addicted to alcohol. I feel that it would be as unwise to censure or condemn the man or woman with an addiction problem as it would be for a physician to censure or condemn a patient with a severe organic illness.

116

In early interviews, I will convey this attitude to the patient, and will mention that I have had a severe problem with alcohol myself and was able to solve it with good, understanding help. I will tell the patient that in my experience personality problems are always different and unique, and that I am aware that no two personalities are alike just because they each have an addiction to alcohol. I do not expect the patient to develop a new personality in solving his problem, but I plan that part of his recovery will consist of accepting himself and being himself. The fact that he was unknowingly running away from himself for many years indicates that a very real struggle lies ahead. It is my belief that the recovering patient can do a great deal about adjusting to the real self once he accepts it, and it is my belief that he can do nothing toward knowing himself until he terminates his drinking. I will point out that the real self is not necessarily a more comfortable self just because he has stopped running away from it, but that those who are addicted to alcohol can eventually acquire greater emotional comfort if they can solve their addiction problem.

The patient who has relinquished alcohol does not become a new man because he has stopped drinking, but he does find that there is a great deal he can do about solving his discomfort after he has stopped running away from it with the aid of alcohol. This was uniquely capsuled by a recovering patient who said to me, "I always thought I was an s.o.b., but now with a year's abstinence I think I am a kind of nice s.o.b." I don't agree with the biblical admonition, "If thine eye offend thee, pluck it out." It seems to me far better to know why the eye offended you, and to get that eye in perspective.

A recovered patient of a number of years was asked to attempt to convey his reactions to our early talks together. He summed it up by saying, "In the first place, you made me feel less guilty and ashamed about my addiction problem. In the second place, you conveyed to me a feeling that you believed I could recover, and in the third place, you conveyed to me that you trusted me." He went on to say that when he consulted me, he was ashamed and guilty about his drinking, that he had lost any belief in the possibility of recovery and that he could not trust himself. He said, "After a number of talks with you, I started to think, 'Here's a man with experience who thinks I can get well. He trusts me, and he does not make me feel guilty and ashamed.' From then on, I started to have a little trust in myself, and to believe it was possible that I could recover. Largely because I was facing my problem, I started to be less ashamed and less guilty about it."

Rapport established on these emotional levels seems essential to me in order to proceed in helping the patient understand the structure of his problem with alcohol.

A recent patient said to me, "I'm OK if I don't drink, but oh, boy, do I go to pieces when I do drink!" When I questioned him about why he drank, he replied, "I don't know, I guess I am an alcoholic." I questioned him further. What did he think an alcoholic was? He replied, "It's just a thing some people are." I questioned him further by saying, "How do alcoholics act?" He gave me a rather stereotyped picture based on hearsay, and some personal experience. He said, "We start covering up about our drinking. We lie about it to our wives or to the boss. We do all kinds of crazy things when we're drinking that we wouldn't do when we're sober. Pretty soon we start needing a drink in the morning to quiet our screaming nerves, and we blame everybody but ourselves for the cause of our drinking."

When I questioned him further as to why he thought he and others behaved in this way, he looked at me in amazement and said, "Because we're alcoholics." He implied that through no fault of his own or of his parents or of his environment, he belonged to a class known as *alcoholics,* and hence was different from other people. This man went on to tell me that he had heard that alcoholism was a disease that you were born with, and that it was some sort of deficiency which made you allergic to alcohol. In other words, he indicated that alcoholism was something that was thrust upon him and that he was not responsible for it any more than a deficient child is responsible for not being able to cope with the challenges met by nondeficient children.

It will be obvious to the reader that this man never considered his addiction problem as something that he could do something about and that until he could accept it as such he had little chance of taking the responsibility of effecting recovery. To begin with, the patient is not aware of why he drinks in an addicted way. It is vitally important that he gain such an understanding, and it will be found that the more understanding he achieves, the more responsibility he will be willing to take for the struggle of his own recovery.

How often I have heard the expression, "Alcohol has a hold on me." It is important to help the patient to reverse this thinking because it is obvious that the patient has a hold on alcohol, and his job is to let go of his hold on it. There are so many different theories about the causes of addiction to alcohol, as well as different approaches to this problem, that no one can blame the patient who has not studied himself and his addiction problem for being confused.

It is my firm belief that the causes are psychological and not physiological, and I have never seen any scientific proof to deny this. Not being a medical doctor, I have no right to even conjecture about the physiological changes that may result from the addiction. This aspect of the problem must be evaluated by an internist, and it is important that such an internist understand our psychological approach and realize the utter futility or even harm that may result from well-meaning attempts to frighten patients out of drinking. The internist's findings must be based on scientific exploration, and the results must be conveyed to the patient exactly as they are. If the findings of the internist are negative, this should be conveyed to the patient. If there is liver damage, neurological, or any other physiological damage, this should be conveyed to the patient and treatment started to arrest or cure the diseased part of the body. It has been my experience that patients appreciate absolute frankness about their physical health and will respond to treatment far better because of this frankness.

In Chapter VI, I said that the theory of this approach is based on showing the patient the structure of his problem and on supplying him with problem-solving tools with which to carve his own recovery. In order to show the patient the structure of his problem, it is necessary to give that problem a name, and the name I have chosen after much thought and deliberation is *an addiction complex.* There are many technical and dictionary definitions of *addiction,* none of which convey to me a true emotional feeling. To me, alcoholic addiction indicates an inability to avoid using alcohol in spite of the fact that it threatens the structure and foundations of the existence of those who use it abnormally. It is obvious, even to the patient without understanding, that life is being curtailed because of his abnormal use of alcohol, that liberty is no longer enjoyed because he has become a slave to alcohol, and that the pursuit of happiness in a normal, healthy way is denied him as long as he remains addicted. The word *complex* is used as defined in *A Dictionary of Psychology*:* "an idea or associated group of ideas partially or wholly repressed, strongly tinged with emotion, and in conflict with other ideas or groups of ideas more or less accepted by the individual."

The psychologist will say that the emotional source of a complex is hidden from the patient. Certainly the reasons underlying addicted drinking are equally hidden from the

*A Dictionary of Psychology by JAMES DREVER. Baltimore, Penguin Books, 1952. Revised edition 1964.

addicted drinker. It is my belief that the intelligent person with an addiction complex knows when he is sober that his whole way of living is threatened by his drinking. He may go "on the wagon" or attempt to limit his drinking because, when sober, he feels guilty and ashamed, and threatened by the last drinking bout, but very soon he finds that abstinence or moderation are in conflict with his tremendous emotional dependency on alcohol. This conflict soon reveals itself in impulses to drink, which he attempts to repress. When the impulses are wholly repressed, we have the phenomenon, which I have mentioned before, called the "pseudo flight into recovery." In such a case, the patient says, "I've learned my lesson. I will never drink again." Or he may attempt to partially repress this conflict by what he calls willpower. "I want to drink, but the big, strong man in me is capable of resisting temptation."

Neither the full nor the partial repression will work because the individual is not facing the true structure of his addiction problem. He is using faulty tools to solve his problem.

In the joint therapy with a psychiatric associate that I have found so helpful, the patient and I largely limit ourselves to the study of the structure of his addiction complex, while my psychiatric associate helps the patient to understand why he developed and built the personality that now harbors the addiction. My job is to supply problem-solving tools to effect the demolition of the addiction complex structure, while my psychiatric associate is helping the patient to understand the faulty structure of his preaddiction personality. This is a far cry from the oversimplification expressed by the wife of a patient. She said, "All he has to do is to stop drinking, and he'll be all right."

In other uses the term *complex* is applied to a neurotic manifestation and, where the reaction is psychoneurotic, the result is incapacitating symptoms, such as compulsive behavior or anxiety states or phobic reactions. Unlike addicted drinking, psychoneurotic symptoms are sick defenses against regressive needs, incompatible with a patient's idea of what he should be like. Addicted drinking, however, actually permits the patient to indulge in regressive needs against which, when sober, he attempts to shakily defend himself. In his case, his repression occurs when sober and takes the form of amnesia; that is, when a person is sober there is no recollection of the deep intoxication experience. My belief is that this amnesia is necessary to protect the personality from the shock it would receive were it aware of the infantile degree of regression that the patient has indulged in by deep intoxication. Sobriety brings back the need of the patient to defend himself from his regressive needs, but the need for defense of regression is soon felt and reindulgence is the order of the day or of the morning.

The pattern seems to be progressive, and the more one is addicted, the more one has the urge to reindulge. Such a patient has only one way to defend himself from his maladjustment to the demands of mature reality—the further defense of regression. I think it is well to emphasize that psychotic or psychoneurotic defense of regression, mental illness. is usually denied the addicted drinker when he is sober. This does not mean that the need for the habitual defense of regression does not persist, but that it persists in symptoms, and that these symptoms reveal themselves in drink impulses. When the patient is able to grasp that drink impulses are regressive needs, he starts dealing with these impulses as emotionally sick manifestations that he is trying to understand and solve.

In helping the patient to understand the many facets comprising the structure of his addiction complex, the first step is to show him that his emotional dependency on alcohol is abnormal and cannot be compared with the normal "dependency" his friends and associates may have on alcohol. Many of those who have consulted me have told me that prior to undertaking treatment, they had again and again determined to drink in a limited, social way, in the manner of their nonaddicted friends, but that these attempts eventually resulted in deep intoxication followed by nervous reactions the next day which could be quieted only by more alcohol or drugs. Without knowing it, the patient in attempting to drink in moderation, is denying his addiction complex. Hence, the first step toward recovery depends on the patient's ability to accept his problem as an addiction.

In dealing with patients, I tell them that they are giving up the most important thing in their lives when they give up alcohol. They will frequently protest or object to this statement, assuring me that they love their wives, children and careers far more than they love alcohol; yet when they face their problem, it becomes obvious to them that they were losing the love of their wives and children, or losing their jobs or their professional careers because of their manner of drinking. This realization brings home to them the tremendous dependency on alcohol which they have attempted to deny for so long.

This book might be said to be a testing ground to see if a patient who reads it can identify his or her addiction problem with the thinking that I have tried to outline. There will be many who will be unable to identify their problem with this text, and for these, other treatment approaches should be recommended.

Among the approximately five million addicted drinkers in the United States, it is ridiculous to expect that each will respond favorably to the same treatment plan. Because addicted drinkers develop an infinite number of forms of personality maladjustments, the causative factors are never going to be identical. The addiction complex developed by each person does, of course, have like symptoms, but the reason for this maladjustment rests on an individual's unique personality. The preaddicted personality structure will in certain cases be so incomplete or so malformed that a reeducative approach such as I have attempted to outline would be useless. My associates and I have long since stopped looking for the universal panacea, the cure for alcoholism, and have realized that the treatment approach and its effectiveness will depend on the study of each personality involved.

One of the first steps in treatment are the evaluation interviews, during which my psychiatric associate and I study the patient's personality and, after comparing our individual findings, make up our minds as to the right approach for that particular patient. We frequently use psychological testing given by our psychology department. Such testing is not, as many patients think, an abstruse evaluation that gathers dust in the files of the psychiatrist. The results of psychological testing are shared with the patient and help to begin generating the understanding of himself.

In regard to this approach, we do not feel that you can make a patient face a problem any more than you can make a patient recover, but you can frequently lead a patient, through understanding, to wish to face and solve his problem. The more carefully the personality is studied, the better we will be able to approach the patient and give him this understanding of his problem.

If a patient has reached the point where he wishes to undertake treatment, he frequently asks us, "How long should this treatment be?" We have long since discarded any arbitrary figure of number of treatment hours or length of hospital stay because we have found from experience that different patients are not going to respond to treatment in a like manner. For instance, some patients seek help and at first are unwilling or unable to grasp the gravity of their addiction problems. Such inadequate response may take many interviews before the patient is able to see and face the structure of his addiction problem and be willing to seek help.

There are so many variables in an addiction complex that we must get to know the patient and assess his response to treatment before we have any right to plan an overall program tailored to fit a given patient's needs. In helping many patients accept their problems, patience is frequently a downright necessity. Once a patient has accepted his need for treatment, we still do not know how well or how badly he is going to respond to it. Therefore, we must be guided in our decision on the length of treatment and the length of stay in our hospital by the patient's ability to cooperate with us. In other words, the patient writes his own timetable by his response or lack of response to our help.

Some patients, in the minority, have been able to respond to outpatient treatment with no need for a preliminary period of hospitalization, while most frankly admit the need for hospitalization before they can even grasp the significance and meaning of our approach. One thing I am convinced of is that a period of complete abstinence is an absolute necessity before the patient can grasp the meaning of this approach and apply himself to it. Generally, the patient needs a period of hospitalization with careful and understanding medical and nursing help as the first step toward his struggle for recovery.

Many of those who consult us come from great distances and because of this, treatment must be tailored to fit these circumstances. Such a patient from two thousand or more miles away should be prepared to stay a lot longer than the patient who lives in the vicinity or who can commute in a matter of an hour or two.

As I have pointed out, those who consult us do so on a voluntary basis and are admitted to an open hospital. By *open* I mean that there are no barred doors, the patient is free to come and go or to leave entirely if he wishes, and the burden of treatment is put on the interviews with a psychiatrist and me rather than on the hospital. There are, of course, simple rules in the hospital and the patient is expected to abide by them. Occasionally, we have a patient who consults us and comes to our open hospital, but is unable to respond and cooperate. In such cases, it soon becomes obvious that the patient is going out of the Institute and getting drinks, and I will tell him that he is wasting his own time and money, I will explain to him that he temporarily needs more support than we can give him in our open hospital, and I will suggest that he get this support in our closed hospital in order to make the break with alcohol. If he is willing to do this, I explain to him that we will be glad to readmit him to the open hospital when he and the physician in charge feel he is ready to benefit.

I have always worked on the theory that if you treat people like children, they are very apt to respond like children. If, on the other hand, you treat them as adults, you give them a chance to respond in an adult way and I believe that in treating people like adults, you get far better response than any other way.

Let us say that a patient has accepted the fact that he has an addiction complex and that he wishes to understand it in order to be able to deal with it. The first thing I will touch on is that for a long while he is going to have a great deal of conscious as well as unconscious resistance to recovery, and in order to familiarize the patient with this, I have him study and discuss with me some seventy-five notes dealing with resistance to recovery that has been encountered by many hundreds of patients who have consulted me over the years. The purpose of this approach is to help the patient learn to distinguish the emotional symptoms that have been supporting his addiction problem. It is all very well to generalize and say that addiction to alcohol is a sick way of facing reality or of not facing reality, but this is only a generalization and in no way describes the intricacies of an addiction problem that has taken possession of the patient.

These notes were the idea of the late Richard Peabody, who very generously turned them over to me to use in my work with those who consulted me. Though these notes show great understanding of the rationalizing process that persists long after a period of abstinence has been brought about, they are written in a somewhat pedantic style; that is, like the teacher lecturing the student, and they savor of the "mind over matter" school wherein the intellect is commanded to dominate the emotions. This approach is foreign to my thinking, as I stress the importance of understanding the emotions that prompt the impulses to drink. My thinking is not "get thee behind me, impulses," but rather, "get right out in front so that I can look at you, understand you and deal with you in a way that will not cause my destruction."

Deliberately, I have left the notes largely as they were written by Peabody in their pedantic style. I do this with a purpose. For instance, the note is read over with the patient, and I point out and dissect with the patient certain emotional aspects of words that are used that I feel are out of date, and I will also try to make it clear to the patient that the intellect is not in command of the emotions that make him want to drink. The reverse is true. The intellect is subservient to the emotion that demands alcohol. Hence, the insidious process of rationalization. The crux of the matter is to help him change the emotions. I suggest to the patient he rewrite these notes in his own language as they pertain to him and his own addiction complex under whose sway he has been for many years. I have seen these notes serve a very useful purpose in helping patients to gain understanding of their addiction complex as well as in familiarizing them with the persistence of drink impulses in spite of the fact that they may have formally gone on record as wishing to solve their problem. The notes also give the patient a feeling of participation. He feels at long last that he is doing something about understanding and solving his problem. Let me give the highlights of some of these notes.

The first note asks the patient to study exhaustively the things that have motivated him to seek treatment. The second note makes it clear that unless recovery becomes the most important thing in the patient's life, he has very little chance of solving his addiction problem. The third note tells of the importance of the patient's using food—candy, tea, coffee, or soft drinks—in the early phase of self-weaning from alcohol. Some deprivation feelings can be lessened by nonalcoholic oral gratification.

Suggestions to drink, due to identifying with situations or people are discussed in some detail. The burden of protecting himself from destructive suggestion rests with the patient. Once the patient has terminated his drinking and is under treatment, I refuse to make decisions for him. I will point out, however, in the early part of treatment, that it is wise for the patient to anticipate situations which are apt to prompt drink impulses and help him to build up in advance defensive measures against such suggestions as he may encounter.

In the fourth note, addiction to alcohol is compared to nonaddicted drinking, and I explain that it has been my experience that once a patient has developed an addiction complex to alcohol, a readjustment is impossible unless the patient accepts not-drinking as a way of life.

Other notes point out many of the resistances toward not drinking that the patient is apt to encounter in his struggle for complete recovery.

Another note is straight from the shoulder and shows the patient how the regressive influence of his addicted drinking has made him start behaving like a spoiled child; that is, he must have the mood that he wants when he wants it, and immediately. The importance of being truthful with those who are trying to help him is emphasized. The importance of self-honesty, far more difficult, is also emphasized. Socrates said, "Know thyself." It seems like common sense that the patient should know the part of himself that turns to alcohol.

Another note is headed, "Giving Up Drinking a Personal Problem," and it explains to the patient that his actions must in no way be contingent on the conduct of others. For instance, sentimental reasons for giving up alcohol, such as, "I am doing it for my wife," are fatal though well-meaning, as are promises. Such motivation for recovery is unconscious projection of dependency needs—the very needs that addiction thrives on. Hence, the patient is encouraged to give up alcohol for one reason alone—to save himself from destruction.

Because of the layman's lack of understanding of the addiction complex, it is pointed out to the patient that he may receive unintelligent advice from his friends. The countless excuses that a patient has been in the habit of using prior to treatment are discussed in great detail and analyzed in a number of the notes. It is pointed out that the patient has been running away from uncomfortable feelings within himself, and these feelings, differing to some extent in each patient, are discussed in detail both with my psychiatric associate and with me.

The inevitable unhappiness that follows addicted drinking is discussed and related to the patient's actual experience. It is pointed out that due to the addiction complex, which thrives on living for the moment, the patient will find it necessary to make a real effort to live beyond the moment. He is struggling to develop the capacity to deal with tension rather than run away from it.

The patient has really built up an addiction-conditioned response to his own emotions; hence, it is necessary for him to attempt to counteract this by building up nonaddiction-conditioned responses which are legitimate defenses against regression. I suggest to the patient that every time he encounters an impulse to drink, he thinks it through to what would be the inevitable consequence.

One note points out that the patient is really learning how to treat himself, and that it is necessary to share this new self-treatment that he is practicing with somebody who understands it professionally. Changes in environment, because they can be emotionally upsetting, should be discussed. The danger of fatigue in the early part of treatment is discussed because it can so often be used as an excuse for turning to alcohol.

The importance of sustained action in order to solve an addiction problem is stressed. It is pointed out that periods of abstinence, important as they are as a preliminary to recovery, are not the be-all and end-all of the addicted drinking problem.

Because a patient has been under the sway of an addiction problem for many years, he must learn to crawl before he can walk, and walk before he can run. He is growing out of a regressive way of life when he relinquishes alcohol.

Anticipation of what a given patient may run into in his struggle for recovery is discussed in great detail. The patient is forewarned of the danger of dropping his guard after he has been through a trying situation which he has been able to handle without turning to alcohol. Because of the possibility that a patient may relapse after he has sought professional help, it is pointed out to him that he may use this possibility as an excuse to have a relapse in the future. The unconscious resistance to recovery and some of its manifestations are discussed in other notes.

Overconfidence and cockiness are discussed. The patient is trying to build up a justifiable self-confidence which he can only do by relinquishing alcohol. Cockiness, which is childish overconfidence, and misplaced self-assurance, can be extremely dangerous. The importance of keeping up his self-respect, not only in matters pertaining to alcohol, but in other fields of life, is stressed. The tie-up of sex drives and alcohol are discussed.

It is pointed out that the initial purpose of drinking, which was to obtain a pleasant state of mind, is now impossible because of the addiction complex. The danger of a flight into pseudo-recovery is stressed. The analogy is made that the wound must heal from the inside out, and the surface must not be glossed over so that the infection remains within. Preaddicted drinking is discussed and compared to the period of addicted drinking.

It is pointed out that relinquishing alcohol created an emotional vacuum, and that the importance of filling this vacuum slowly and carefully with other interests and other things can be an important aspect of recovery. Because many patients, due to their addicted drinking, find themselves in bad situations such as threatened divorce or loss of a valued position, it is pointed out that it is futile to wait for ideal conditions to begin treatment. The time to face an addiction problem is right away, no matter how uncomfortable the situation or the environment may be.

It is stressed that disagreeable emotions such as anger, worry and sorrow can serve as good excuses for drinking, but that it is equally true that pleasant emotions can also serve as excuse mechanisms for reindulgence.

I explain that all people have fluctuations in mood swings (Fig. 1). The abnormal drinker has attempted to influence these swings with alcohol (Fig. 2).

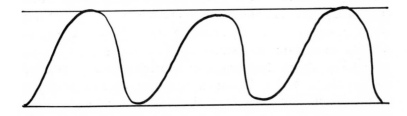

Figure 1. Normal mood swings (parallel lines indicate normal swings).

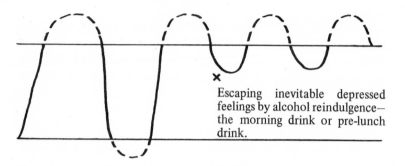

Escaping inevitable depressed feelings by alcohol reindulgence—the morning drink or pre-lunch drink.

In Figure 2, I attempt to show how the abnormal drinker can extend the upswing by drinking. This is indicated by dotted lines above the normal brackets. This euphoria is followed by depression, illustrated by dotted lines below the normal brackets. Soon the addicted drinker learns that he can temporarily abort the depression by reindulgence in alcohol so that in a drinking episode lasting for days he escapes depressed feelings each time he reindulges in alcohol. Due to the habit of inducing elation by the use of alcohol as escaping feelings of depression, the patient has a real struggle in getting his mood swings back into normal brackets. It is pointed out that the conflict about drinking will not disappear just because the patient has sought professional help, and that it will take a long while and much self-treatment before conflict eventually disappears.

Another note points out that discontent is frequently the first stage of achievement, that a person who is discontented and facing his discontent will eventually do something about solving it if he has given up the old narcotic way of running away from it. Because most of the people I see are potentially above the average of capability, this is pointed out to them, and it is shown that just because they are intelligent, if they can solve their drinking problem once and for all they usually can become effective, contributing people after recovery.

The tendency of self-pity in a person with an addiction complex is discussed, and the immaturity of this emotional response is dissected and analyzed. The dynamics of treatment are gone into so that the patient is well aware of what he is striving for in treatment, and of what he expects to get out of it.

There is a tendency in some patients in the early part of treatment to be disagreeable and irritable in their home environment. This is discussed by the patient when he encounters it in himself. He soon sees that much of his irritability is a disguised form of sulking because a toy has been removed. It is stressed that his approach to treatment is time-consuming, and that if the patient is looking for any quick cure he has come to the wrong source.

Because giving up anything is negative, it is stressed that the positive aspect of recovery should be borne in mind; namely, what the patient acquires because he has been willing to relinquish alcohol. If I did not believe that the patient would get more out of himself and out of life because of his recovery, I would frankly not be interested in this work.

The importance of a healthy, aggressive attitude toward gaining pleasure is emphasized. For instance, the person with an addiction problem reasons, "I can't have any fun if I don't drink." If he stops drinking, his attitude should be, "I'm not going to drink. Now let me see how much I can contribute, as well as gain, in pleasure from this or that situation."

These are a few condensations of the notes that are not only an effort to show the patient the countless rationalizing processes that he has been using prior to facing his problem, but which also point out to him that the rationalizing process will continue a long time after abstinence and that this rationalizing process is apt to become more circuitous as it is projected into the future. An illustration of this is a patient who was very earnest in wishing to face and solve his problem. After a considerable amount of treatment, he brought me the following thought that he had had: "I can accept my not drinking now, and for many years into the future, but when I am an old man and retired, I envision sitting in my library, occasionally having a Scotch and soda, and my grandchildren will come into this library and chat with this pleasant old gentleman." Later on in treatment, I reminded him of this thought that he had had, and he said, "Isn't it extraordinary? In the very library that I am talking about, I saw my father-in-law drink himself to death. My children, his grandchildren, were afraid to go into the library because the old gentleman was so frequently drunk, and they were very frightened of him. Why did I never see this picture and compare it to my old age?"

I am sure that the layman who has never had an addiction problem would find it very hard to grasp that alcohol can have such a tremendous hold on the emotional life of those who are addicted to it. The nonaddicted layman thinks in terms like this: "If alcohol was ruining my life, I certainly would quit." Because it is that simple to the nonaddicted, their tendency is to become angry with a friend or a relative because they have not sense enough to stop ruining their lives with alcohol. For this reason, I doubt if the layman can ever have any real understanding of the complexities of an addiction problem. Hence, the recovering patient must be prepared for this lack of understanding. In time, society, his friends and relatives will accept the fact that he has solved his drinking problem, but I doubt if they will ever have any understanding of the emotional growing pains that the recovering patient needed to go through on the way. Because of the lack of understanding of those close to the patient, he feels alone in his recovery struggle and professional help by those who are trained to know what he is going through alleviates much of this feeling. The patient is not just relinquishing alcohol for good and all, important as that is. He is also effecting an emotional maturing process which is absolutely impossible unless he relinquishes alcohol. Anything is better than the patient destroying himself with alcohol, and if the problem can be arrested by whatever means, it is all to the good. This approach is not aimed at merely arresting the problem, but at solving it with understanding.

These notes are intended to help the patient learn to distinguish the emotional symptoms that were the support of his addiction problem. It is all very well to say that addiction to alcohol is a sick way of facing reality or of not facing reality, but this is only a generalization and in no way describes the intricacies of the addiction problem that has taken possession of the patient.

The structure of this addiction problem and all the crooked thinking that supports it must be analyzed and traced back to discomfort and anger in the individual. The patient is actually like a medical student who is making a study of the syndromes, that is, constellation of symptoms that distinguish one disease from another disease. In this case, he is studying the symptoms which he encounters as he struggles to make a readjustment without alcohol. The important thing is that at long last he is recognizing that for many years he had emotional syndromes that were supporting his addiction problem, and now with understanding he is endeavoring to deal with them in a nonregressive way.

What are these resistances to recovery that the patient may encounter? Very simply put, they are impulses to drink, and the habit of supporting these impulses with rationalization, "I drink because," and the because is "because I am uncomfortable." The rationalization may be prompted by feelings of anger, frustration, disappointment, physical discomfort, or more subtle feelings of insecurity or inferiority, feelings of shame and so on. As the patient gains understanding into his addiction problem, he gradually becomes aware that other people have a great deal of emotional discomfort at times, and he questions himself, "Why are they dealing with it in a nonregressive way, and why do I only know how to deal with it in an addiction way?" And so it is gradually dawning on him that the rationalizations that supported his addiction to alcohol made it seem to him as if the cause of his drinking was coming from his external environment. With understanding, he begins to see that it was life that he was running away from, or maturity or its demands, but that he was really running away from his inadequate response to the burdens of maturity and life. As he gradually begins to see that these drink impulses are actually protests against his own emotional responses, he has a good chance of now dealing with them with more understanding and more effectiveness.

Dr. Kenneth Appel defines psychotherapy as "helping people to handle their feelings, behavior and motivations more effectively." In applying this definition to the addicted drinker, it is obvious that his feelings are extremely uncomfortable, his behavior, when drinking, is abnormal and self-destructive, and the motivations that caused him to drink abnormally are hidden from him. In order to effect communication between the patient and us, access to the patient is limited in the early part of treatment to the feelings of the patient. The patient has sought help because of his feelings. He has reached the point where he senses, "I don't seem able to live with alcohol, and I don't seem able to live without it." This is the breakdown point that frequently motivates many intelligent men and women to ask for help.

It is my belief that it is unwise in the early part of trying to help a patient to dwell on the behavioral aspect of the patient's problem, or to dwell on the motivation that caused the addicted drinker to turn to alcohol. The old adage, "First things first" seems to apply, and the first conflict the patient shares with the therapist is, "One part of me wants to drink, and another part of me wants to stop drinking." This should be considered as an emotional weaning phase of treatment. We have been asked for help by the patient, and in order to render the right kind of help, we should have a very good understanding of the patient's feelings that follow the withdrawal from alcohol, and we should understand and convey to the patient that cessation from drinking for which he has received skilled medical treatment, usually in a hospital, is only a first and very small part of the total emotional weaning process that he has to go through. If the patient, as frequently happens, brings up past intoxicated behavior because there is a good deal of shame connected with it, I will tell him that generally this behavior was a symptom of his addiction problem, and it is my belief that this destructive behavior, whatever it may have been, will cease with his understanding of it as he effects a readjustment without alcohol. If the patient wishes to investigate the motivations of why he developed an addiction problem, I will discuss with him broad theoretical views such as I have outlined in this book, but I will emphasize that in the first part of treatment this aspect of his problem is of secondary importance, although it may be extremely important later in his treatment with my psychiatric colleague.

In the early part of treatment, the real emphasis should be in trying to understand the immediate feelings of the patient rather than what caused them. To put it bluntly, the patient and those of us who are trying to help him in the first part of treatment have a full time job in understanding his immediate feelings and these feelings are largely influenced by alcoholic conflict.

I believe I am being practical and realistic in taking this approach. The addiction problem is destroying the patient and his feelings about it are decidedly abnormal. It seems obvious to me that the patient's emotionally sick feelings about himself and his addiction problem must be dealt with primarily, and these sick feelings do not clear up when the patient has stopped drinking. To expect abstinence from alcohol to change the patient's feelings about alcohol is ridiculous in the light of the emotional dependency on alcohol which existed for many years prior to the time when he sought help.

I believe that treatment should be viewed as aimed at a dual purpose: first, to help the patient understand the abnormality of his feelings toward alcohol; and second, to strengthen his ego. He cannot strengthen his ego as long as he is indulging in alcohol, and without insight into how very sick and maladjusted these feelings are toward alcohol, he has little chance of effecting recovery. Taking a long-view perspective of treatment, we see the interplay of the strengthening of the ego going hand in hand as the patient emotionally relinquishes his abnormal dependency on alcohol.

To get back to Dr. Appel's definition of psychotherapy, I have indicated that the first step is getting people to understand their feelings toward alcohol and helping them to handle these feelings without resorting to drinking. Where this has taken place satisfactorily, my psychiatric colleague will find that the patient is more accessible to gaining further insight into the motivations that caused him to become addicted. The amount of psychiatric treatment that is necessary will vary widely, depending on each patient's personality. Some will need a great deal more than others.

It is fortunate that at long last people are gradually becoming aware of the importance of the emotional segment of the total personality, and beginning to realize that when this segment becomes so painful that it is interfering with their adjustment, they can turn to skilled psychiatric treatment. I have been fortunate, indeed, and greatly influenced by my close association with three men, Dr. Earl D. Bond, the late Dr. Edward A. Strecker, and Dr. Kenneth E. Appel, who have taken great strides in educating the public as well as their fellow physicians in the importance of helping people in the early stages of emotional disturbance, before they became chronic. My hope is that this same relationship is taking place in people with drinking problems, who dare to recognize the symptoms and seek help in the early phases of their addiction.

Another treatment approach, that can be helpful for certain patients, I call *formal relaxation.* I will first explain to the patient why his use of this measure is indicated and why it may prove helpful, by saying, "You have become dependent on alcohol in order to relax yourself. You have been using it both as a tranquilizer and as a narcotic, without being aware of it. Therefore, I am going to give you a more healthy way to help yourself relax." I will emphasize that my giving them this relaxing exercise is unimportant. The important thing is that they get in the habit of giving it to themselves, and I have seen patients become quite dependent on this autorelaxation, and use it for their entire lives. In my way of thinking, there is nothing wrong with being dependent on something that is constructively helping you to solve your problems. On the other hand, I should feel greatly at fault if patients were to become dependent on me to relax them. Hence, the importance of my stressing that they carry the burden of relaxing themselves more and more as they find this a beneficial tool toward facing and solving their problem.

Thirty-five years of experience in this field have convinced me that in the initial phase of treatment, patients need a great deal of support if they have an addiction problem. If they are terminating an acute episode in a hospital, they get this support medically and from the nursing staff, and they get it from me and my associate in therapy. As the patient makes progress, the important thing is to keep feeding him back support as we feel that he is gaining enough integration of personality to accept self-support rather than external support. I am sure that well-adjusted parents of children sense this intuitively. They are quite ready to support their children emotionally, but gradually, step by step, they are withdrawing their support and turning it back to the child because they sense that the child can now support itself. So, too, with the person who is abnormally dependent on alcohol and addicted to it, we who are trying to help him must sense when the patient is ready to accept more self-support and less external support. Even in the very early part of treatment, I will not make decisions for patients. I will, however, discuss with them in great detail their own decisions, and ask them to take into consideration whether or not their decision is influenced by their abnormal dependency on alcohol. If a patient makes a decision and it happens to be a wrong one, he then can take the full responsibility for the wrong decision. On the other hand, should I make the decision for him, he is not really responsible for that decision and could always use me as a scapegoat because the decision happened to be wrong.

I have tried in this book to indicate a dynamic approach to helping a patient face, meet and solve an alcohol addiction problem.

INDEX

141